A Roman Hoard of Silver Jewellery Found in the Lower Danube Region

Objects from a Zagreb private collection

Remza Koščević

BAR International Series 2289
2011

Published in 2016 by
BAR Publishing, Oxford

BAR International Series 2289

A Roman Hoard of Silver Jewellery Found in the Lower Danube Region

© R Koščević and the Publisher 2011

The author's moral rights under the 1988 UK Copyright,
Designs and Patents Act are hereby expressly asserted.

All rights reserved. No part of this work may be copied, reproduced, stored,
sold, distributed, scanned, saved in any form of digital format or transmitted
in any form digitally, without the written permission of the Publisher.

ISBN 9781407308661 paperback
ISBN 9781407338484 e-format
DOI https://doi.org/10.30861/9781407308661
A catalogue record for this book is available from the British Library

BAR Publishing is the trading name of British Archaeological Reports (Oxford) Ltd.
British Archaeological Reports was first incorporated in 1974 to publish the BAR
Series, International and British. In 1992 Hadrian Books Ltd became part of the BAR
group. This volume was originally published by Archaeopress in conjunction with
British Archaeological Reports (Oxford) Ltd / Hadrian Books Ltd, the Series principal
publisher, in 2011. This present volume is published by BAR Publishing, 2016.

BAR titles are available from:

BAR Publishing
122 Banbury Rd, Oxford, OX2 7BP, UK
EMAIL   info@barpublishing.com
PHONE   +44 (0)1865 310431
FAX   +44 (0)1865 316916
www.barpublishing.com

TABLE OF CONTENTS

Antescriptum   ii
Introduction   iii
The Silver Hoard   1
Postscriptum   16
Abbreviations   17
Bibliography   18
Catalogue   23

ANTESCRIPTUM

The flip side of the human ability to create is revealed by constant negatively motivated impulses, which threaten the survival of the fruits of human creativity on the part of their very creator. Various degrees of damage and destruction to the cultural heritage extend unrecorded throughout all of human history. Archaeology itself is often the later witness to destruction that has taken place in all epochs and all communities, without reference to their degree of development and civilized manners. It is paradoxical that one of the earliest documented acts of vandalism – the demolition of the temple in Jerusalem – was carried out on the part of the Romans more than two millennia ago, although this ethnically coloured term first began to be used to denote perceived "barbarian" behaviour in attacks on the Roman Empire.

Our age has also been marked by more than occasional destructive attacks (Bamyan, Babylon, Kabul, National Museum of Afghanistan, Cairo, Egyptian Museum, etc., etc.) which continue to fill the otherwise considerable dossier of uncivilized acts. The sacrosanct absolutes of the aesthetic value of cultural items set up from as early as the Renaissance today seem dangerously weakened. Despite insistence on their complete exclusion from any possible damage in situations of conflict, achieving the status of an untouchable monument of the past seems to give ground before the once again awoken iconoclastic, globalistic, and other modern forms of conquest and violence.

Faced with ominous threats in the near future, the imperative necessity arises of the urgent registration of every available piece of the past – not merely immobile monuments, but also mobile one – so that they would not slip through our controls and disappear irretrievably.

INTRODUCTION

The past few years have seen increased efforts in publishing both old and modern archaeological collections, whether from state institutions or privately owned. Objects in private collections represent a significant proportion of the total archaeological finds that have come to light. An essential shortcoming that is almost always present and which leads to their less valuable situation in the sense of scientific evaluation refers to the lack of key data about the conditions in which they were discovered. Without such basic information, these are "silent" objects that speak only partially and indirectly. However, after a period of exhaustive elaboration of various kinds of finds both from museum collections and from systematic excavations, representing authentic scientific sources, the archaeological profession has finally matured to the phase of accepting the inclusion of objects from private collections and has increasingly dealt with such items. Their lack of original data is abundantly compensated for by the supplementary or new information offered in relation to types and variants, and also variations in form, decoration, and function, and in this sense their importance is invaluable.

A special category exists among archaeological finds in terms of hoards composed of precious metals, which in addition to their cultural importance also have a significant artistic value. Hoards in a certain manner may surpass "ordinary" finds from everyday life due to their history or background that was caused by some exceptional situation. The character of their composition is also varied, just like the reasons for their deposition, as well as the level of information that they offer, all dependent on the contents themselves. In a certain sense, they are small collections with compositions based on religious, sentimental, or other feelings, or were determined merely by knowledge of the material value of the contents, whose selection was decided by chance. Most were accidental discoveries, with no possibility of verifying the intactness of the uncovered material. The established practice is to publish them in monograph form, with the material subsequently being included in synthetic works that encompass a specific geographic region or chronological period, illuminating the creative achievements of a given time and place. One such hoard is presented in this study.

THE SILVER HOARD

One private numismatic collection in Zagreb, Croatia was found to contain a group of silver items, which has all the characteristics of an authentic Roman hoard, including the usual scarcity of information about the circumstances of discovery and the specific location. Only the following is available in terms of relevant information about the hoard: this chance find comes from the Lower Danube region and was found in a pottery vessel removed from the earth at a depth of approximately 1.5 meters. The type, name and specific or at least approximate location of the site of discovery remain unknown, along with the type and form of the vessel into which the objects were places, and it is not absolutely certain whether the hoard represents an intact complete unit, or if it once perhaps contained other items.

The hoard consists of 46 items made from a silver of high purity with a very little admixture of other metals. No analysis was undertaken of all the silver. The partial analysis carried out using x-ray fluorescence only on parts of the hook and eye on the braided wire necklace no. 19 (Fig. I) noted the presence of small inclusions of gold, lead, tin, copper, zinc, and iron, with traces of cadmium, chrome, palladium, and titanium. Although its composition has not been entirely verified, the very appearance, colour, and shine of the silver reveals the uniformity of its fineness, with a possibility of only minimal differences in percentages. All of the objects are in an excellent state of preservation (Fig. II, Fig. III), and some of them are without a patina (Fig. IV).[1]

The Lower Danubian basin, the region where the hoard was discovered, in the Late Hellenistic period was considered a territory with a non-homogenous population that included: in the west the Illyrians with the most prominent tribe of the Autariatae, east of them the Thracians with their main tribe of the Triballi, and to the north of these – above the Danube – the Dacians and Getae and the Celtic Scordisci, all stabilized in their positions in the 3rd century BC. In the Roman period, this was the region from which the provinces of Moesia, Thrace, and Dacia were formed.

Despite the insufficient essential data, whose lack intensifies the complexity of questions concerning the discovery of its cultural and chronological context, the hoard is sufficiently interesting to attract professional attention. The reasons for such interest transcend the framework of standard contributions in the sense of supplementing previously known material and – because of certain to date poorly known objects that the hoard contains – reach a level close to that accompanying rare discoveries.

The contents of the hoard

The hoard contained solely silver jewellery elements, some of which were gilded, and consisted of 7 filigree pendants and 9 beads, 1 section of a filigree wire necklace, 2 pendants with annular circlets, 12 torcs, 10 bracelets, and 6 crescent pendants. The total weight of the hoard is over 1200 grams. The precise weight of the silver cannot be determined because of the presence of underlying bronze platelets on example no. 4 and beads and the remains of   wooden rods on examples nos. 42 - 44.

---

[1] The cleaning of the objects, along with minor restoration and the cited testing of the silver purity on one piece, was carried out professionally by Damir Doračić, BA (Archaeological Museum in Zagreb). In the photographic documentation recorded prior to the cleaning, islands of green (bronze) patina are visible, mixed with soil in the bracelets, in the spiral twisting of the torcs, and on pendants nos. 42 - 46, where the rear side of individual pieces were almost entirely covered by a green layer. The filigree and granulated objects nos. 1 – 7, nos. 10 – 18, and the woven chain no. 19, all with slight damage but which do not display traces of contact with earth or with the other objects from the hoard, were probably wrapped in leather or cloth prior to being deposited.

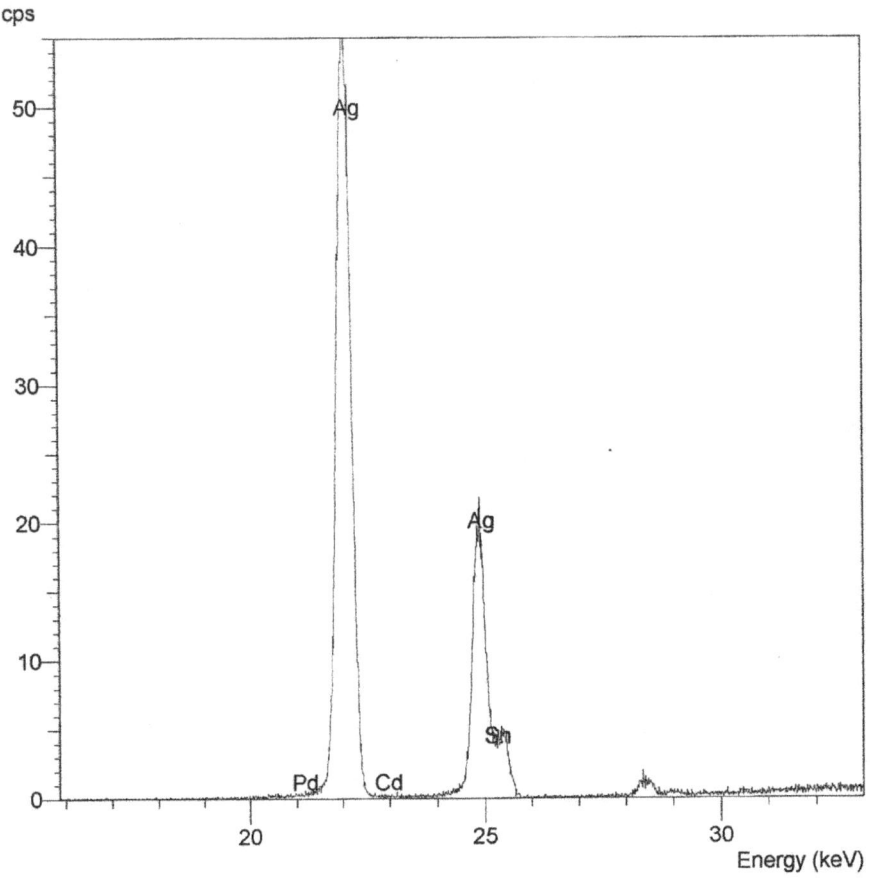

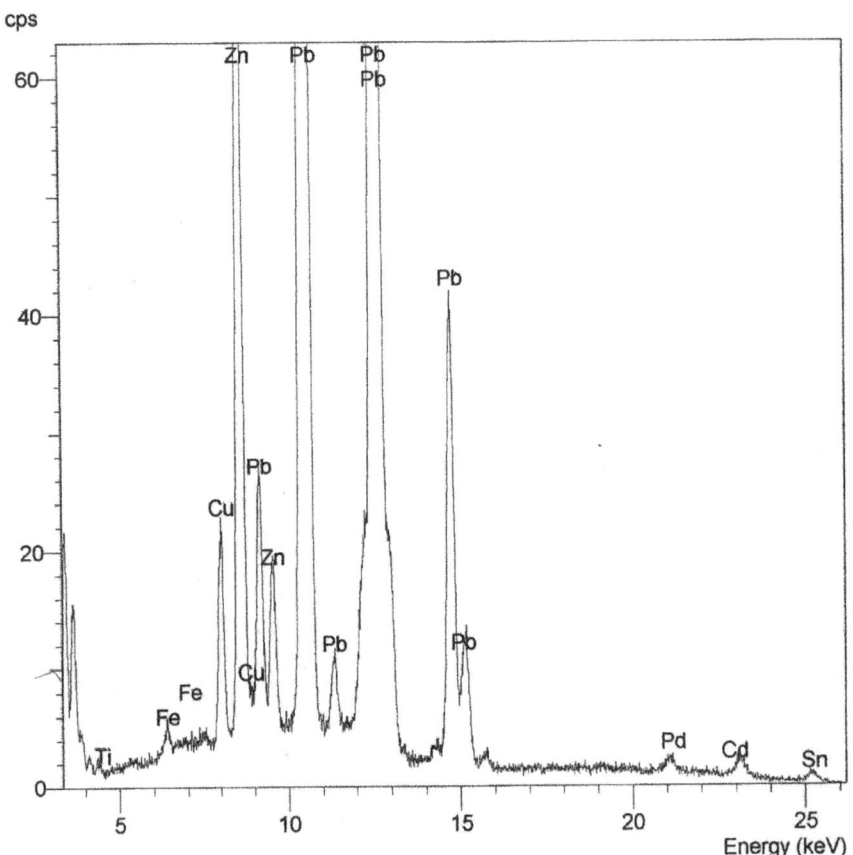

Fig. 1 The results of x-ray fluorescence analysis carried out on certain sections of item no. 19 (the woven chain): A – the hook, B – the cylindrical tubular clamp element

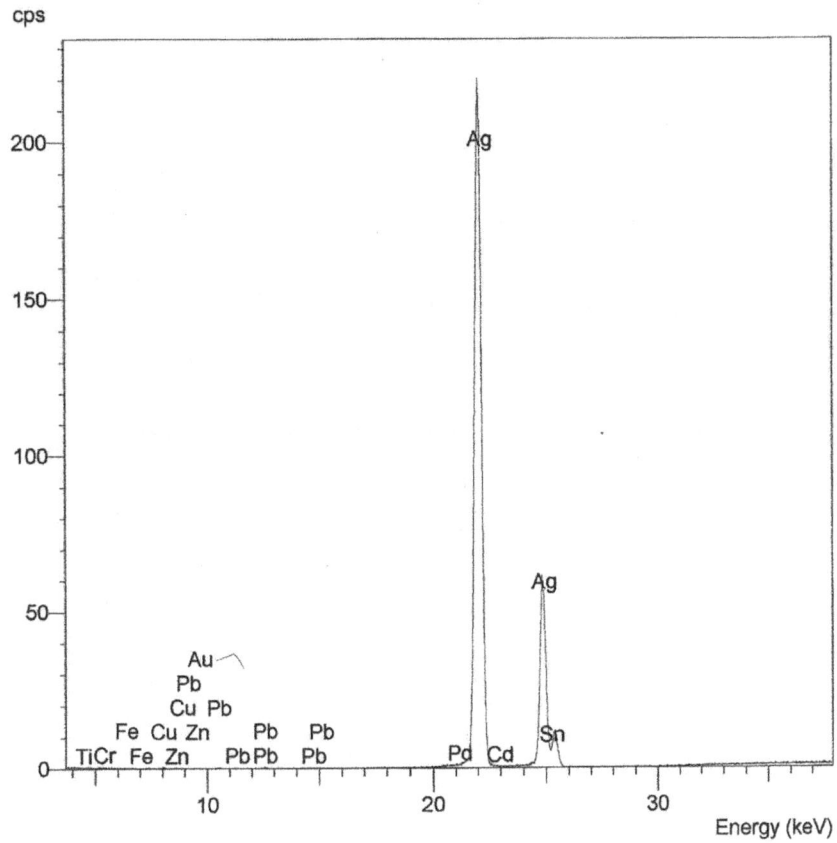

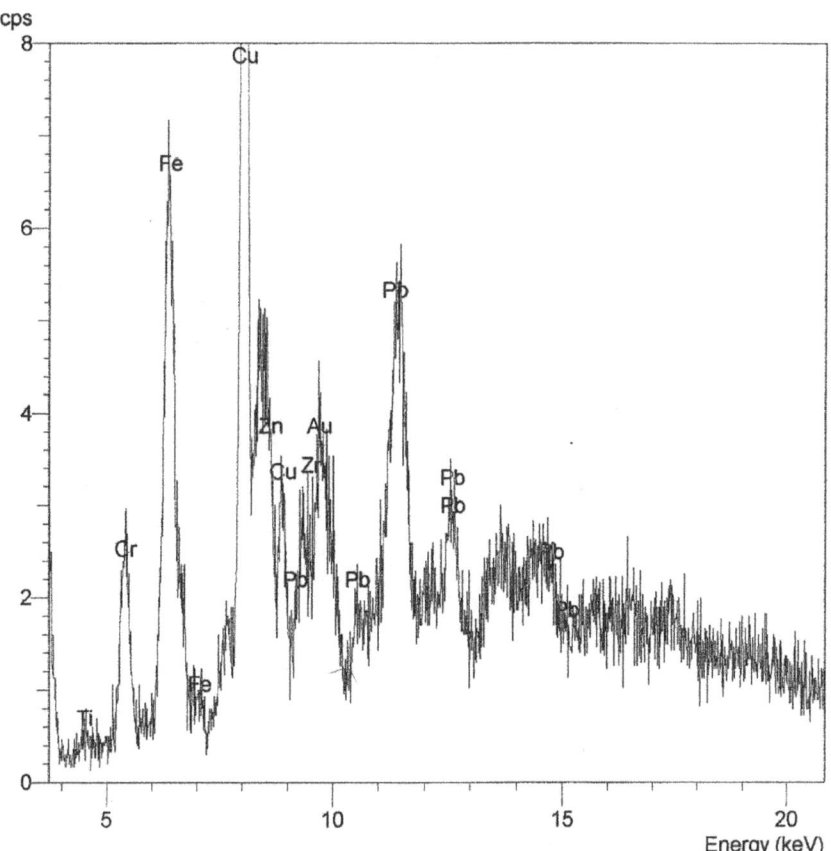

Fig. I The results of x-ray fluorescence analysis carried out on certain sections of item no. 19 (the woven chain):
C and D – one broken-off domed button: both sides (Fig. IV above)

A Roman Hoard of Silver Jewellery

Fig. II The appearance of items nos. 27, 29-31 prior to cleaning

Fig. III The appearance of item no. 42 prior to cleaning

Fig. IV The group of items nos. 1-7, 10-19 without any patina

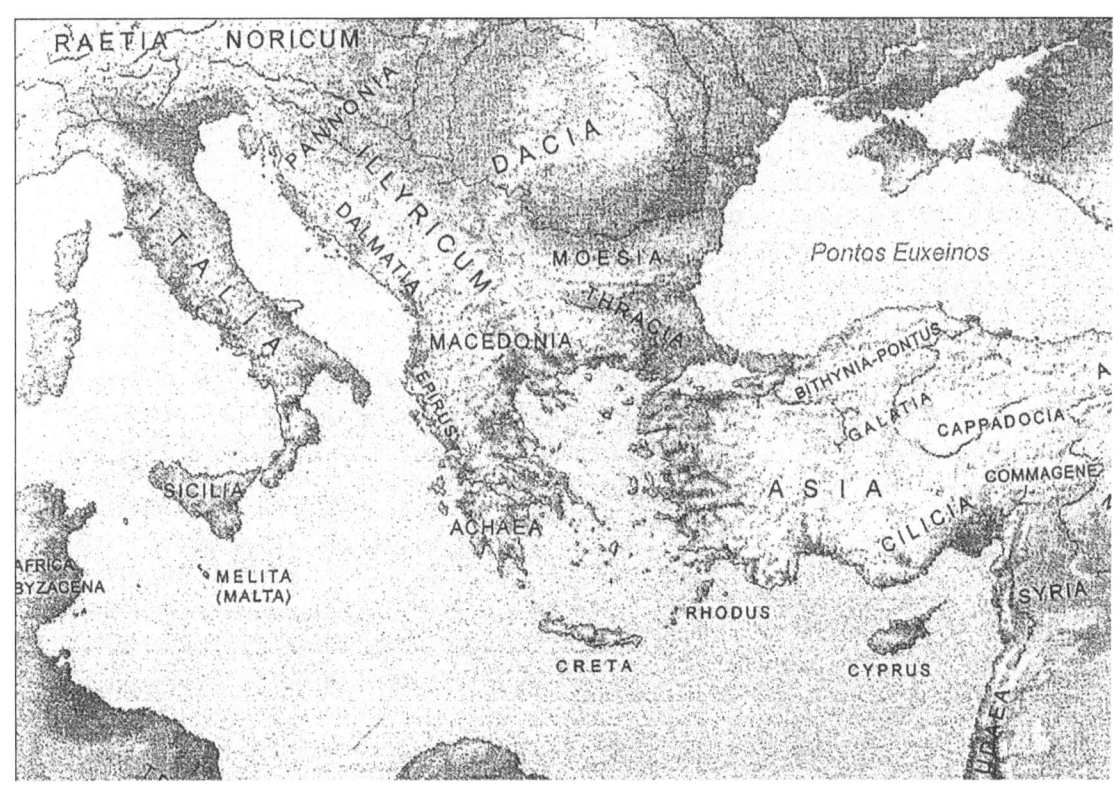

The Lower Danube Region showing the Roman Provinces of Moesia, Thrace and Dacia
(THRAKER I, 311)

Pendants

Of the nine pendants, most were of unusual form and only in the formal sense can they be placed in this category.

Examples no. 1 and no. 2 (Fig. 1a,b; Pl. I. 1, 2) can be classified as classic pendants that could have hung from earrings or – with the aid of another circlet – on a necklace, or they could have been sewn onto clothing. All three purposes are equally possible, considering that the grains on the top of the loop for hanging are omitted, but no specific purpose can be confirmed, as such or an even slightly similar form of figure-eight designs among known examples of jewellery cannot be found.

Examples nos. 3 – 7 (Fig. 2 – Fig. 3; Pl. I. 3 - 7) represent two types of miniature recipients with a handle, which represent isolated, as yet unseen forms of mysterious purpose. These five items – two cylindrical (Fig. 2a,b; Pl. I, 3, 4) and three square (Fig. 3a,b; Pl. I, 5 – 7) – are not suitable for independent standing, but are for hanging. They cannot be associated with any other known type of object, and it is unclear whether they were independent entities or sections of some other larger items. The search for analogies from various epochs and milieus, which encompassed several types of jewellery items of similar dimensions, mostly made from precious metals,[2] gave no directly positive results. The search for comparative analogies was not exhausted with this, but it was considerably reduced. This also refers to the sphere of cults, where neither of the two forms exhibits any interfacing elements with any of the known objects from a religious inventory, whether of western or eastern faiths.

The only cylindrical forms that can be found (R. RAŠAJSKI 1961: 18, 20, Pl. I, 11; S. BARAČKI 1961: 120, Pl. IV, 10) represent double-sided closed barrel-shaped forms, but, with half of the cylinder joined by melting wire above the seam of the juncture, the first of the cited examples exhibits a certain relation to the production techniques of nos. 3 – 7. The square forms cannot be found elsewhere.

The location of the decoration on the containers, which define them as single-sided objects, suggests a position that could be viewed from in front and below, i.e. at the level of the eyes or somewhat above them. This would best correspond to a highly elevated pendant or temple ring, worn on some kind of diadem or forehead band. Such a purpose would also be indicated by the specific curvature of the banded handles on pwieces nos. 3 and 4, which to a certain extent confirms this otherwise unprovable hypothesis. The open top to the container on all five specimens is particularly unusual, indicating a special and unknown content. It must have differed from those with protective qualities common in the Roman period, which were, for example, most often stored in the most popular type of amulets, known as bullae, but which were always closed after placement of the special contents. Along with the idea that further forms of decoration could have been placed in the cylindrical and square containers, it should not be excluded that solid scents or other substances, whose effect would increase with intensive evaporation, could well be in question.[3]

These specimens cannot be defined in terms of cultural allegiance, much less chronologically, on the basis of their form.

Specimens nos. 8 and 9 (Fig. 4a,b; Pl. II, 8, 9) can be classified among pendants in the form of an axe, which, like pendants based on the forms of other tools, were quite widespread among the autochthonous milieus of the Balkan region, the source of their original roots. Pendant-axes appear from the Early Iron Age to the Late Roman period in two basic types with several variants:

---

[2] Outsized examples appear among earrings: conical sheet metal earrings with banded loops, but with closed recipients (M. URLEB 1974: 57, Pl. 20, grave 100, 1; 1975, Pl. 4, 7), filigree earrings of the "*a bauletto*" or "basket-shaped" type, with a cylindrical form also represented (GIOIELLI 1988: 38, 142, br. 60; TROY 1996: 117, no. 125, 126), earrings with a completely closed hoop, made for a different manner of attire (F. R. IŞIK BINGÖL 1999: 68 – 81, nos. 40 – 53), or immense earrings without any part to attach to the ear, which had a funerary purpose (F. H. MARSHALL 1911: 250, 255, 256, Pl. XLIV, 2252, 2256), but all of these, other than the conical ones, feature decorative platelets and not a container. Among pendants, similarly granulated spherical examples can be found, but with a very narrow opening (M. CHŁODNICKI 1996: 41, 42, Fig. 27), and also a cylindrical filigree pendant, but with a covered container that contained an amulet (F. H. MARSHALL 1911: 225, 226, Pl. XXXIV, 2024). Other types that can be cited include a twice-larger filigree pear-shaped flask for perfume, but it has a different manner of suspension with a loop (E. H. MINNS 1965 II: 433, 434, Fig. 326). The cited examples display a certain similarity, but in terms of form and purpose they do not represent even approximate analogies for examples nos. 3 – 7.

[3] In this context, information is illustrative about tablets made from ground iris roots, attributed to traditional Illyrian pharmacology, worn next to the body to overpower the scent of bodily perspiration: A. STIPČEVIĆ 1974: 89.

with a loop for suspension on a narrow or wide platelet, smooth or with surface decoration,[4] or in a simplified form with a platelet that hung from an ordinary opening at the top.[5] They can be seen on bracelets and other jewellery, where they are usually considered to have apotropaic and prophylactic significance (Đ. MANO ZISI 1957: 17, 18, Pl. III, 7, Pl. IV, Pl. IX, 12; ANTIČKO SREBRO 1994: 205, no. 56), but where they almost always have two faces and the appearance of tools, and very rarely the form of a battle axe (K. GSCHWANTLER 1999: 70, 75, Fig. 19).

Pendants nos. 8 and 9, whose circlets have spirally wound ends with a La Tène provenience, but because of massive and lengthy use are not chronologically sensitive, represent a quite rare version of a true miniature axe with a complete set of decoration from the Hallstatt ornamental repertory (M. EGG – C. PARE 1995: 158-160, Pl. 54, 2). The contours are reminiscent of the form of a battle-axe, and given the width of the blade and its line, they fit well into the Thracian milieu, where examples can be found of very old miniature axes with a curved blade, which belong to a Bronze Age context (THRAKER 1979: 77-79, nos. 126-128). Through an additional zoomorphic decoration, such miniature axes are related to Luristan and Caucasian forms, and are defined as cult objects: It is considered that the axe, as a symbol of power, played a similar role in the Thracian world view as it did in the art of Asian Minor (THRAKER 1979: 23).

The miniature axes nos. 8 and 9 could have served as cult objects. Since they have a single face, it should first be suggested that they were suspended from some cult vessel, whose shape would have been based on the form of a situla or ciste (M. EGG – C. PARE 1995: 164-166, Pl. 56, 3), rather than on the handles of a patera (Đ. MANO ZISI 1957: 29, 30, Pl. XX, Pl. XXI), or on a sceptre, which were used in religious ceremonies, or even on flat mounts (L. RUSEVA-SLOKOSKA 1991: 7). On the other hand, these examples could equally be seen as human jewellery, or even as a horse harness element, where axe forms can also be found (THRAKER 1979: 23). As they were discovered as a pair, despite their massiveness and weight, it might be possible to see in them earrings for occasional formal wear.

Considering the archaic shape of the blade and the type of decorative motifs, the miniature axes nos. 8 and 9 should be assigned to the chronological period of the transition from BC to AD.

The closest analogies to the axes can be found in an almost identical example from the site of Ratiaria in Bulgaria, which is dated to the first two centuries AD and defined as an earring (L. RUSEVA-SLOKOSKA 1991: 26, 131, Cat. No. 71): Its plate is somewhat narrower and lacks decoration, while the upper section with the loop is identically designed, and it weighs almost 12 grams.

Beads

The nine identical specimens nos. 10 – 18 (Fig. 5, Pl. II, 10 - 18) are somewhat thick and short variants of cylindrical beads. They were probably threaded on a necklace as spacers, combined with other beads, although they are sufficiently decorative to create an entire necklace by themselves.

Tubular beads were present sporadically but permanently in Mycenaean, Etruscan, Italic, Greek, and Roman jewellery, in various renderings: from sheet metal examples with two or three or up to five or more ring-like protrusions, through spiral wire specimens, to luxurious filigree items.[6] No examples analogous to nos. 10-18 can be found among beads of cylindrical shape, not particularly because of different dimensions, rather primarily because of the atypical manner in which they were made by joining finished ring-shaped elements, which differs from all the cited examples. The closest comparisons for these specimens are the somewhat narrower and longer silver beads from the previously mentioned find from Kovin in Vojvodina from the 1st century BC, which was defined as a Late La Tène silver Dacian hoard (R. RAŠAJSKI 1961: 7, 18, 20, Pl. I, 8), but with somewhat more emphasized Celtic character (CELTI 1991: 484).

---

[4] True miniature axes mostly have a short trapezoidal platelet, which is sometimes specifically elongated: S. BARAČKI 1961: 130, 138, 140, Pl. IX, 20; ANTIČKO SREBRO 1994: 205, no. 56; M. CHŁODNICKI 1996: 17, 34, 36, Fig. 12, 19, 20.

[5] Such flat pendants with an opening in place of a loop are mostly decorated with circle-based motifs: D. POPESCU 1940: 185, Fig. 3, 5; C. S. NICOLĂESCU PLOPŞOR 1948: 23, Pl. II, 11; M. GARAŠANIN 1973: 512, 513, Pl. 115; I. BOGNÁR KUTZIÁN 1975: 36, Pl. V, 1; GOSPODARI SREBRA 1990: 198, no. 141, 142: M. GUŠTIN 1991: 11, 12, Pl. 40, 23, 24.

[6] Such flat pendants with an opening in place of a loop are mostly decorated with circle-based motifs: D. POPESCU 1940: 185, Fig. 3, 5; C. S. NICOLĂESCU PLOPŞOR 1948: 23, Pl. II, 11; M. GARAŠANIN 1973: 512, 513, Pl. 115; I. BOGNÁR KUTZIÁN 1975: 36, Pl. V, 1; GOSPODARI SREBRA 1990: 198, no. 141, 142: M. GUŠTIN 1991: 11, 12, Pl. 40, 23, 24.

Although the tubular beads from Kovin – made of bent sheet-metal with soldered ring-shaped protrusions of beaded and smooth filigree wire – were produced in the usual manner, they are nonetheless sufficiently close to offer an at least relative chronological framework for examples nos. 10-18 still within the boundaries of the BC era.

Necklaces

The necklaces consist of one woven chain, no. 19. (Fig. 6a,b; Pl. III, 19), and twelve neck rings, or torcs, nos. 20-31 (Fig. 7 - 18; Pl. IV - Pl. XV).

The wire chain no. 19 represents one of the most basic forms of necklaces, woven in a form known under several names, such as Fuchsschwanzkette, or link-in-link, or the so-called Isthmion type. The form has a Greek origin, and it represents a standard element in Hellenistic jewellery production. Such necklaces can be found in almost all milieus: Cretan, Asian Minor, Etruscan, Italic, in general somewhat more prominently in the Greek world than the Roman,[7] while they were also represented among Illyrian, Celtic, and Thraco-Dacian jewellery.[8]

Woven chains were particularly popular in communities of the Balkans, where they were worn in female jewellery sets over clothing as semi-necklaces to connect a pair of fibulae or as chains hung from the ends of fibulae,[9] often supplemented with pendants.[10] But such a combination of clothing clasps and chains should not be considered as a distinct attribute of the Balkan region, since pendant chains that connect the shoulders of fibulae also appear in female British-Celtic Roman period jewellery, naturally with pairs of fibulae of the type worn there.[11]

Their wide diffusion means that the woven chain necklaces are culturally neutral in and of themselves, while certain distinctions can be made to a certain extent on the basis of the shape of the clasp[12] or other specifically formed parts.

Specimen no. 19 exhibits mixed details on the clamped ends and the sections for fastening that reflect various influences. It was outfitted with an unproportionally massive clasp with a bird-shaped hook. Both in terms of dimensions and the zoomorphic beak-like stylized hook, the clasp is most analogous to one on a woven chain that comes from the Dacian region: The chain represents part of a silver hoard from Aţel, which was dated by coinage to the 3rd century AD, but was probably created much earlier (I. H. CRIŞAN 1959: 359, 360, Fig. 2, 5).

The domed buttons with five small arcade elements, soldered onto both parts of the clasp on chain no. 19 – which were organically related through the filigree decoration to the group of objects nos. 1 - 7 and nos. 10 - 18 (Fig. 1 - Fig. 7 and Fig. 5) – are identical to the circular filigree caps with four small arcades on bracelets from the hoard from Šabac in Bosnia: The hoard was defined as an Illyrian-Roman treasure from the second half of the 2nd century AD (J. PETROVIĆ 1941: 16, 23, Fig. 3 b).

The decoration of the cylindrical clamp ends of necklace no. 19 does not have the frequently seen wavy meander (G. BECATTI 1955, Pl. CI, 387), but instead is composed of rows of elongated triangles. Such angular wavy lines can be noted first in the 4th century BC among Greek influenced jewellery, on the terminals of a silver chain with snake protomes, used to join the shoulders of a

---

[7] They were made from precious metals, and the number of wire braids, i.e. the thickness of the chain, varies: F. H. MARSHALL 1911: 145, 146, 216, 315, Pl. XXII, 1463, Pl. XXXIV, 1959, Pl. LVIII, 2720; G. BECATTI 1955: 164, 186, 193, 202, Pl. XXIX, 157, Pl. LXXIX, 317, Pl. XCIII, 364, Pl. CXVII, 431, 432; A. BÖHME 1974: 12, Fig. 12; S. G. MILLER 1979: 24, 48, Pl. 8, Pl. 22.

[8] Where they belonged to the period of the 5th century BC to the 1st century AD: ILIRI I DAČANI 1971: 164, 165, no. D 188; GOSPODARI SREBRA 1990: 188, no. 138; J. V. S. MEGAW – M. R. MEGAW – J. W. NEUGEBAUER 1997: 723, Fig. 3.

[9] Various combinations of pectoral jewellery are documented by images on a large number of monuments from central and eastern Bosnia: C. PATCH 1909, Fig. 70 – 72, Fig. 124; I. ČREMOŠNIK 1963, Fig. 8; 1964, Fig. 11.

[10] Among the pendants, those in the form of a specifically shaped ivy leaf stand out in terms of numbers: I. ČREMOŠNIK 1963: 118, Fig. 10; A. JOVANOVIĆ 1978, Fig. 164; ANTIČKO SREBRO 1994: 243 – 249, nos. 121, 122, etc. Leaf-shaped pendants and fibulae of the so-called anchor type (Ankerfibeln), which appear along with woven chains in Bosnia, Dalmatia, Bulgaria, and Romania (E. PATEK 1942, Pl. IX, 7, 9; L. RUSEVA-SKOLOSKA 1991: 54, 151, cat. no. 135; I. ŠOPOVA 2004: 341, no. 343; I. H. CRIŞAN 1959, Fig. 3) derive their origins from Thracian and Illyrian traditions.

[11] The shoulder fibulae belong to the British version of the trumpet brooch: A. BÖHME 1974: 20.

[12] The form of the clasps on the woven chains ranges from simple sheet metal cylinders with an ordinary hook and loop (F. R. IŞIK BINGÖL 1999: 124, 125, 158, no. 131, 132, 168), to luxurious filigree clamps with snake-head endings (D. POPESCU 1940: 184, 187, Fig. 4; CROAZIA 1993: 118, no. 107), or with additional decorative panels (ANTIČKO SREBRO 1994: 221, 246, 248, nos. 84, 130, 131, 134).

pair of fibulae with a distinctive shape (F. H. MARSHALL 1911: 335, Pl. LXVII, 2845, 2846).[13] Such fibulae appear in several variants in the Balkan region, and they have been found in Greece, Bulgaria, Serbia, Macedonia, and Bosnia and Herzegovina. Angular wavy lines also appear on the conical terminals from the previously noted silver hoard from Kovin from the 1st century BC (R. RAŠAJSKI 1961: 8, 20, Pl. I, 7), which also contains the previously cited partial analogies to the cylindrical beads.

The details of the composite parts of necklace no. 19 revealed Dacian and Illyrian formal components. The motif of angled wavy lines would indicate an earlier Balkan decoration of a remodelled, straight-line meander, present on jewellery from the last century BC, the period to which the terminals and clasp on specimen no. 19 would belong, while the woven chain itself could be later.

Considering that its original length is not certain, the chain with loops could have served originally for connecting the shoulders of fibulae, and after the clasp was added, secondarily as a necklace. An only slightly longer chain, with identical but somewhat shorter tubular terminals with a rounded wavy line, from the Samokovska region in Bulgaria, dated to the 2nd-3rd centuries AD, was classified as a necklace (L. RUSEVA-SKOLOSKA 1991: 151, Cat. no. 134).

Neck rings – or torcs – are considered a jewellery type characteristic of the Celts or Gauls, but they can also be found among other populations, particularly those considered barbarian, but also those of the Middle East.[14] The origin of torcs has not been fully explained. They appear in great numbers at Western European sites from the Bronze Age to the Roman period.[15] They were worn from an adolescent age, and protective characteristics were attributed to them through the symbolism of the circle, which were further strengthened by the protomes of various animals located on the ends. They also played a role in the religious sphere, as an attribute of the gods, to whom golden torcs were sacrifices, sometimes together with gold coins. Such hoards are known from almost all western Celtic regions,[16] and on the basis of the unsuitable weight of some examples in these hoards,[17] it can be presumed that such examples were worn only temporarily on special occasions. Golden torcs were a prerogative of sovereignty, while at the end of the 4th and in the 3rd centuries BC they gained a distinct reference to both a tribal and noble origin.[18] At the transition from the 3rd to the 2nd centuries BC, torcs began to decline, both in numbers and in the preciousness of the metal, the ring became thinner, and the ends became less emphasized (M. Y. DAIRE 1991: 247).

The importance that the Roman attributed to torcs as war trophies meant that they were included among military decorations – as donna militaria – and in this role they acquired smaller dimensions, and probably a distinct shape, and one or more examples were worn suspended from the shoulder (M. DEIMEL 1987: 67).[19]

Torcs appeared in significant numbers in the Balkan region from as early as the Early Iron Age onwards, but in different, somewhat less luxurious versions. In the Illyrian and Thracian milieus they most often have a spirally twisted ring with smooth terminals curved outwards or with a discoid design (M. GARAŠANIN 1973, Pl. 101, Pl. 104, Pl. 106; THRAKER 1979: 93, 94, 127,

---

[13] These are fibulae of the Štrpci type (named after the eponymous site of Štrpci near Goražde in Bosnia), which are also known from Trebeništa, Radolišta, Čurug, and other sites, and extend from the 4th century BC to the Hellenistic period: F. H. MARSHALL 1911: 335, Pl. LXVII, 2841, 2843; G. BECATTI 1955: 92, 93, 197, Pl. CV, 396; M. GARAŠANIN 1973: 512, 513, Pl. 112; BLAGO 1975: 10, 35, nos. 159, 165; THRAKER 1979: 130, 131, no. 261; PRAISTORIJA 1987, Pl. LVI, 5; L. B. POPOVIĆ 1994: 27, 174, no. 219, etc.
[14] On Persian depictions, they are worn by ancient female goddesses and warriors in cult chariots (H. STIERLIN 2006: 32, 75, Fig. 32, 75).
[15] In versions from bronze and silver to gold, and in variations from simple ones with hooks or buttons to the top-rank form "a tamponi" with complicated relief decoration, see: G. BECATTI 1955: 170, 209, 212, Pl. XXXVI, 207, Pl. CXXXV, 475, 476, Pl. CXXXIX, 493; CELTI 1991: 199, 202, 207, 219 ff.
[16] They have been documented in Germany, Switzerland, Belgium, and Britain, and are most often dated from the 4th century BC, extending to the 2nd and 1st centuries BC, but it remains unclear whether the reason for the deposition referred to the torcs as a specific form or merely the gold from which they were made: C. ELUÈRE 1991: 355; R. and V. MEGAW 1996: 182, Fig. 308 – 310.
[17] 17 The iron, gold plated torc from Trichtingen in Germany, utilized as an offering to some (water) deity and hypothetically placed in the 3rd century BC, weighed 6.5 kg: O. H. FREY – M. SZABÓ 1991: 480.
[18] They are not rarely found in female graves with rich grave goods in the Rhine valley and Champagne, where their presence is attributed to hierarchical reasons: C. ELUÈRE 1991: 353; P. ROUALET 1991: 149; R. and V. MEGAW 1996: 126.
[19] On the funerary stele of M. Caelius, centurion of the 18th legion, discovered at Xanten and dated to the very beginning of the 1st century AD, the deceased is depicted with a corona civica on his head and a complete set of military decorations: along with the large phalerae on the chest, he also had armillae on the arms, and a pair of torques attached to the shoulders; the shoulder torcs differ considerably from the neck ones and have snake heads: M. JUNKELMANN 1986: 81, Pl. 24.

no. 164, no. 249). Among the Dacian forms, examples can be found with banded ring and also with clasps (DACI 1997: 155, 353, no. 62, no. 840, no. 841), as well as examples with an open ring with serpentine ends (R. FLORESCU 1997: 89).

Of the twelve torcs with an open ring, nos. 20 - 31 (Fig. 7 - 18), all of them are spirally twisted, except for the first torc no. 20 (Fig. 7; Pl. IV, 20), which has a smooth-edged ring. Their diameters range from ca. 12 to over 20 cm, and all are fully preserved, except for the incomplete example no. 29 (Fig. 16 a, b; Pl. XIII, 29). The rings of the large torcs, no. 30 and no. 31, could be closed with an additional part.

In terms of the shape of the ends, which as a rule are hammered flat, several types with variants exist: with snake head terminals (nos. 20 - 22, Fig. 7 - 9; Pl. IV, 20, Pl. V, 21, Pl. VI, 22), rounded ends (nos. 23-26, Fig. 10 - 13; Pl. VII, 23, Pl. VIII, 24, Pl. IX, 25, Pl. X, 26), banded ends (nos. 27 - 29, Fig. 14 - 16; Pl. XI, 27, Pl. XII, 28, Pl. XIII, 29), and widened ends with a straight cut edge (no. 30, no. 31, Fig. 17 - 18; Pl. XIV, 30, Pl. XV, 31).

Suitable analogies for some examples are difficult to find among the torcs from the Balkan region. Examples with massive, flowing protomes are more frequent among the torcs with snake heads, such as a silver piece from Dacia (TRÉSORS 1994: 122, no. 212), and the same is true of snake-like bracelets (M. GARAŠANIN 1973: Pl. 110, Fig. 1).

The stylized snake heads on examples nos. 20 - 22 (Fig. 7 a, b – 9 a, b) are closest to those on the flat ends of Hallstatt bracelets with Illyrian characteristics from Mramorac in Serbia and from Čurug in Vojvodina from the 6th and 4th centuries BC, respectively (PRAISTORIJA 1987, Pl. LVI, 2; GOSPODARI SREBRA 1990: 181, 182, 197, no. 127, 3, no. 141, 3, 4; ANTIČKO SREBRO 1994: 159, no. 15). Such or similarly designed snake protomes were the sources from which specimens nos. 20 – 22 were derived.

Examples nos. 23 - 26 (Fig. 10 -13), in terms of the form of the ends, with the exception of no. 26, and in terms of the neutral decoration of incisions and stamped rows, have no close parallels, and the decorative motifs are in general based on Hallstatt ornamentation. The same is true of the isolated example no. 28 (Fig. 15 a, b).

The decoration of torc no. 27 (Fig. 14 a, b), seems to be somewhat similar in terms of the same motifs and their arrangement to that on the ends of the massive silver bracelet from the Dacian hoard from the site of Sîncrăeni in Romania, dated to the 1st century BC (D. POPESCU 1958: 178, Fig. 23, 2), and the central row of dots as seen on example no. 29 (Fig. 16 a, b), is the only decoration on the – also damaged – silver spiral bracelet from the Dacian hoard at the site of Herăstrău from the 1st century BC (DACI 1997: 342, no. 788).

Numerous parallels can be found for the massive torcs with trapezoidal widened ends and a small circular opening, nos. 30 and 31 (Fig. 17 a, b and Fig. 18 a, b), all of which come from the Bulgarian region where it appears that form originated, evolved, and had a lengthy continuity. Earlier golden examples in the form of spirally twisted bracelets, one from the site of Skrebatno near Blagoevgrad, from the 5th century BC, with punched decoration (THRAKER 1979: 108, no. 198; L. KANOVA 2004: 147, no. 203), and the other from an unknown site, with undecorated ends closed off by a spiral wire with 6 coils, from the 4th century BC (L. KANOVA 2004/1: 300, no. 282), have wide ends with irregular edges, while the later silver torcs, dated to the 2nd and first half of the 3rd centuries AD from Čauševo (L. RUSEVA-SKOLOSKA 1991: 41, 135, Cat. no. 86, 87), have elongated, narrowed ends and within their edges punched and engraved decoration, which extends around the circular hole. Examples no. 30 and no. 31 are closer to the earlier specimens in terms of the form of the ends, but closer to later ones in terms of the decoration, and can be assigned to the 1st century AD. The same chronological determination would also apply to the other torcs, nos. 20 - 29.

Bracelets

The relations between the bracelets with open ends, consisting of ten examples, nos. 32 – 41 (Fig. 19 - 24; Pl. XVI, 32 - 37, Pl. XVII, 38 - 41) are different, as in contrast to the torcs, most have zoomorphic designs.

On the zoomorphic specimens with a banded, slightly rounded exterior ring, three different stylizations appear, two of them snake-like, represented each by one example, no. 32 and no. 33 (Fig. 19 and Fig. 20; Pl. XVI, 32, 33), while the third zoomorphic variant was represented by four examples, in fact two pairs, nos. 34 – 37 (Fig. 21 - 22; Pl. XVI, 34 - 37). The remaining four bracelets, nos. 38 – 41 (Fig. 23 a, b - 24; Pl. XVII, 38 - 41), belong to the simplest form and lack decoration.

The exterior diameter of the bracelets ranges from ca. 6 to ca. 7 cm.

Bracelets with snake-headed ends are very ancient, quite widespread, and very long lasting, and their origins arise from the Aegean basin. They were worn in identical pairs on both arms, with a distinct meaning in social ranking. They also were included in sets of military awards.[20]

Snake-headed bracelets appear in numerous variants in the Balkans, which were mostly worked with a great deal of plasticity and with a massive ring (L. B. POPOVIĆ 1994: 156-162, 163-179), with the exception of multiple spiral bracelets with a specific style characteristic for the Dacian region (TRÉSORS 1994: 125, no. 214; DACI 1997: 344, no. 802).

Banded concave hoops, such as on the zoomorphic bracelets no. 32 and no. 33, in general are more rarely found on open-ended bracelets with a single span,[21] and otherwise it is difficult to find adequate parallels. The schematic stylization of the ends on no. 32 (Fig. 19) undoubtedly comes from the same basic design as that on the silver bracelet from Kutina near Niš, dated to the 2nd century AD (ANTIČKO SREBRO 1994: 241, no. 117), and relatively close analogies for this variant are offered by the silver bracelets from the Bulgarian sites of Nikolaevo and Čauševo, dated to the 2nd-3rd centuries AD (L. RUSEVA-SKOLOSKA 1991: 159, cat. no. 160, 161). Specimen no. 33 (Fig. 20 a, b) has a direct analogy in an identical bronze bracelet from the site of Moțăței in Romania, dated to the span from the second half of the 2nd to the first half of the 3rd centuries AD (G. CANTACUZINO 1948: 317, 318, Fig. 3).

The zoomorphic stylistic workmanship on specimens nos. 34 – 37 (Fig. 21 - 22), devoid of any expressiveness whatsoever, is difficult to connect directly to a specific animal species,[22] although it does seem that it would best correspond to some kind of reptile. According to the exterior contours, it does appear that in fact this would be a simplified derivation of one of the numerous stylistic versions of formation of a snakehead, with a sharply emphasized transition to a narrowed neck. A certain comparative connection for this type of snake protomes can be established with the massive cast silver bracelets exhibiting considerable plasticity from Radolišta, from the 5th century BC (L. B. POPOVIĆ 1994: 164, 165, nos. 184, 185): Their ends have a different appearance, but they were manufactured in the same manner of modelling on the basis of grooved lines. In terms of the design of the protomes with the emphasized "ear" segments, the form also has points of contact with the massive bracelet from the find from Gornji Vakuf from the 2nd-3rd centuries AD, which is placed in a Thaco-Illyrian context (I. ČREMOŠNIK 1963: 119, Fig. 12).

The bracelets with a smooth circular-sectioned ring, nos. 38 – 41 (Fig. 23 - 24), and somewhat narrower or thicker blunt ends, have numerous direct parallels in examples from Romania, where they can be followed from the Hallstatt and La Tène epochs to the advanced late Roman period (M. MOGA 1948, Fig. 2, 1, 2, 4, 7; D. POPESCU 1948: 38, Fig. 1, 5, Fig. 7, 3; I. H. CRIȘAN 1959: 366, Fig. 2, 8, 9; V. DUMITRESCU 1968: 209, 210, Fig. 19, 3, 4).

As was the case with the majority of torcs from the hoard, the majority of bracelets do not offer a reference to a specific form. Part of them display chronologically insensitive stylistic or technical elements, inherited from the earlier strata of the Balkan region, some of them rooted in the Hallstatt tradition and retained into the Roman period. The cited analogies do not offer a basis for placing bracelets nos. 32 – 41 in a narrower chronological framework within the 1st century AD.

---

[20] They are depicted in that capacity on a fragmentary stele from Burnum, where both the spirally twisted torcs and bracelets have snake-headed ends: B. ILAKOVAC 1976: 159, 160, Fig. 2.

[21] Rounded hoops are more common on bracelets with double spans and on those that mimic the entire body of a snake: CELTI 1991: 234; J. (ÖZ) DEDEOĞLU 1993: 36; MAGIE 1996: 71, 72, nos. 82, 83.

[22] Among the zoomorphic bracelets with sculptural ends that represent fantastic and realistic animal heads in the Greek, Roman, Celtic, and Scythian jewellery repertory no model for such a formal solution can be noted: F. H. MARSHALL 1911, Pl. XIII, 1205 - 1207, Pl. LXIII, 2881; L. FRANZ 1940, Pl. VII; G. BECATTI 1955, Pl. XCV, 367, Pl. CXLI, 498, Pl. CXLII, 499.

Crescent pendants

Sheet-metal crescent-shaped or lunula pendants nos. 42 – 46, Fig. 25 – 30, Pl. XVIII, 42, Pl. XIX, 43, Pl. XX, 44, Pl. XXI, 45, 46) represent a special group that is combined from several components: pairs of joined cylindrical tubelets and three-part (the main outside crescent with an interior crescent and a further interior leaf-shaped element) and two-part (exterior crescent and interior leaf-shaped element) pendants, connected by wire chains and loops. The first specimen, no. 42, with two pairs of short tubelets is somewhat larger than the rest and was hung between the tubes, while the others consist of two pairs, the first pair suspended from loops running through somewhat longer tubes (no. 43 and no. 44.), while the other pair merely hand from loops (no. 45 and no. 46.).

Fig. V The remains of wooden reinforcement rods from the metal tubes on items nos. 42-44

These were items intended for decoration, but two possibilities exist in terms of their purpose: jewellery for people or for horses, and it is not simple to decide. Placed one next to the other, with the largest pendant in the middle (Fig. 30), and in the present state of preservation, they form an unwieldy row, too lengthy for jewellery to decorate a human chest. A hypothesis that they formed a belt set is negated by the central pendant, as this central position would in fact cover the section of the belt for buckling, but even in cases of the buckle being placed to the side or the back, the problem of its impracticality remains, considering the protruding cylindrical tubes. The solution seems more convincing that these were pendants for horse equipment. Not merely in terms of dimensions, but also because of other characteristics, this set would best correspond to a chest or perhaps forehead decorative jewellery for a horse, where the tubes filled with wooden strengtheners (Fig. V) would have been fixed to the skin, and the pendants would have hung freely without overlapping: they would have jangled when the horse ran, and this sound effect was also one of the specific elements of the metal harness parts, where blue beads were also not rare.

Research into Roman cavalry equipment, based on elements that can clearly be distinguished from the equipment of draught horses, has shown that it was mainly borrowed and reflected the ethnic variety[23] that arrived through the influx of foreign mercenaries[24] during the Principate (A. K. LAWSON 1982: 132).

The thesis that Roman horse equipment was taken over from the Celts at the time of their entrance into the forces of the Roman cavalry is based on several confirmations, and one of the more indicative is offered by lunular pendants resembling boar tusks, which have been found in both Celtic and Roman contexts, and whose further development on Roman equipment was independent and unconnected to the Celtic original (M. C. BISHOP 1988: 98, 107, 116, 154, Fig. 48, 9 f.).

The lunula, otherwise one of the earliest type of amulets with considerable apotropaic powers, and popular throughout the world of antiquity, was worn most often as jewellery on necklaces as a pendant of this different, distinctive form. On the other hand, the crescent shape is considered the earliest Celtic-Roman type of pendant on horse harnesses, from which the later bird-shaped[25]

---

[23] According to present knowledge, it appears that in the first half of the 1st cent. AD Gallic bridles were in use in the Roman cavalry, while from the 70s Thracian versions began to be utilized; and the term "sella scordiscus" for a type of saddle known from as early as the middle of the 2nd century BC certainly has an ethnic overtone: A. K. LAWSON 1982: 145.

[24] The institution of a mercenary military service represents a phenomenon manifested among the Celts from as early as the 4th century BC, and as mercenaries Celts fought on Sicily, and in Greece, Egypt, and Asia Minor: M. SZABÓ 1991: 333; R. and V. MEGAW 1996: 123. Along with the Celts, the Thracians were also a significant mercenary element; mercenaries appeared in considerable amounts in the Roman army after the First Punic War: M. ROSTOVCEV 1974: 186, 262.

[25] Connected to the Celtic Mars through the attribute of a bird: M. C. BISHOP 1987: 118, Fig. 6, 1, 2.

and leaf-shaped[26] forms were derived. The lunula pendants from harness straps from the pure western Celtic milieu[27] have a different shape than the Roman ones, which were almost always positioned as chest decoration.[28] In the second half of the 2nd century AD, the number of pendants on harnesses declines, but the lunula type was retained in the following centuries (A. K. LAWSON 1982: 153, Pl. 54, 1, 2).

Pendants nos. 42 – 46 can rightfully be placed in the eastern Celtic or Thracian milieu of forms, and chronologically classified to the second half or at the latest to the end of the 1st century BC. In this limited scope, a final inclination to their use for decorating horses – in relation to the previously discussed possibilities – is offered by the completely different appearance of the Thracian chest jewellery for humans, the pectoral, which regularly was in the shape of large laminate panels (THRAKER 1979: 28, no. 176, 29, no. 175, 93, no. 163, 107, nos. 194-196). On the other hand, such a determination of the purpose of pendants nos. 42 – 46 is not merely not confirmed by Thracian finds of harness decoration, but is almost disproved: most of these decorations were manufactured according to a completely different, primarily animalistic paradigm from as early as the 5th century BC onwards (THRAKER 1979: 112, no. 207; G. KITOV 2003/1: 30 – 33, Fig. 33 – Fig. 38; L. KONOVA 2004/1: 291 – 293, no. 249, no. 250). It is paradoxical, however, that the only directly comparative Thracian example (also chronologically concurring) with identical pendants was defined as a belt set (I. ŠOPOVA 2004: 345, no. 352h).

In relation to the western European simplified massive cast bronze production of metal pendants, the crescent form on pendants nos. 42 – 46 would typologically correspond in form to the variant Bishop–9h, and the leaf-shaped form to variant Bishop–8f (1988: 347, Fig. 4, 5-11).

Pendants nos. 42 - 46 have direct analogies in bronze examples of the western version from the first half of the 1st century AD, discovered at Magdalensberg, some of which also correspond in terms of dimensions (M. DEIMEL 1987: 311-313, Pl. 82, 2, 4, 6, 9, Pl. 83, 1).

On the basis of the individual composition and ornamentation, as well as the type of metal, the objects nos. 1 – 46 (Fig. 33) as a group in general display a close relationship to silver Thracian hoards, and though certain elements with Dacian silver hoards, with other admixtures, but are also partly atypical in comparison to them.

This hoard contains three somewhat integrated units in terms of execution: a filigree group nos. 1 – 7, 10 - 19 (Fig. 31), a group forged from bars with engraved decoration nos. 8, 9, 20 - 41 (Fig. 32), and a group embossed in sheet-metal nos. 42 - 46 (Fig. 30).

The first group contained examples whose purpose – on the basis merely of their shape – could not be defined.

It has already been stated that examples nos. 1 – 7 (Fig. 1 – Fig. 3) represent a new, isolated phenomenon in the Danubian region, but this does not apply completely to their decoration. This group further consists of beads nos. 10 –18 (Fig. 5), and the domed buttons on the clasps of necklace no. 19 (Fig. 6). All of the objects from the group are decorated with silver filigree and granulation, applied to silver, partly gilded sheet-metal.

Their filigree is difficult to attribute directly to one of the main or even secondary forms of this

---

[26] Observations are interesting about variants of leaf-shaped pendants in the form of oak leaves, whose decoration – viewed upside down – can be seen as pairs of animals, most bird-shaped, heraldically placed around a central vessel: M. DEIMEL 1987: 96, 97, Pl. 83, 2, 3. This is a very ancient figural motif, present in both the Early and Late Iron Age (CELTI 1991: 150, 175; M. EGG – C. PARE 1995, Pl. 54, 2) and particularly in Gallic ornamentation (with pairs of dolphins or panthers and with a vessel or some other object in the centre): S. REINACH 1894, no. 340; E. ETTLINGER 1975, Pl. 13, 15, 17; CELTI 1991: 175. This motif can also be traced in the period of Late Antiquity, in terms of frequent appearances on belt mounts and buckles: H. BULLINGER 1969, Fig. 17, 18, 21 ff.
[27] The Late La Tène bronze lunulae from Altenburg (J. WERNER 1953: 48, Fig. 6, 1 – 3), have arms that branch and tend to bend in a more dynamic manner, recognizable as a typical formation of ends on various Celtic creations.
[28] Where they were placed as independent pendants or in combination with other pendants: C. CICHORIUS 1896 – 1900, Pl. XXI, Pl. XXXI, Pl. XXXVII, Pl. XXXIX, Pl. LXV, Pl. LXXI, etc. However, on reconstructions of the typical equipment from the Tiberian-Claudian and Flavian epochs, lunulae do not appear, the decoration instead consisting of bird-shaped and three-branched leaf-like pendants, such as can be found on the famous harness sets from Xanten and Leiden: I. JENKINS 1985: 142, 151, Figs. 1, 15; M. C. BISHOP 1988: 113 – 115, Figs. 29 – 31.

specific manner of decoration, developed in the artistic production of individual cultures.²⁹ It is rather characterized by a timidity and absence of a strict ornamental design, along with the presence of a certain dose of horror vacui, as shown by the overcrowded decoration, particularly on the square containers nos. 5 – 7. One of the details that can be culturally defined to a certain extent on some of them – rosettes made of wire with a granule in the centre – which can be noted on early Italic gold jewellery from the 6th century BC, to some extent discovered in Magna Graecia (F. H. MARSHALL 1911: 136 – 139, Pl. XX, 1414, 1416, 1420), reflects a direct influence from Magna Graecia or Greece itself, brought to the Danubian region together with the filigree technique.³⁰ However, the already somewhat unskilled craftsmanship of the filigree decoration distances these examples from the true products of Magna Graecia and moves them towards objects of a similar level of production created in the Danubian region.

This primarily refers to the still existing golden and lost silver find with Celtic characteristics from Szárazd-Regöly in Hungary, dated to the 2nd – 1st centuries BC (CELTI 1991: 354; R. and V. MEGAW 1996: 167, Fig. 267), with which the filigree group exhibits complete similarity in details: elongated filigree wires arranged in triangles on the conical terminals of a golden necklace, identical to those on no. 3 and no. 4. (Fig. 2), the edges at the juncture of the two halves of the golden beads were worked in the same manner from spirally twisted wire as the rosettes on nos. 1 – 2 and nos. 5 – 7 (Fig. 1 and 3), while identical cones coiled from wire with a grain at the top, more discreetly present on the bottoms of nos. 3 and 4 (Fig. 2a), can be compared to a version more similar to conical protrusions on bracelets made in true filigree (N. MAJNARIĆ PANDŽIĆ 1970: 89, Pl. XXV, 6; J. TODOROVIĆ 1968: 144, Pl. XXI, 9), which belong to the eastern Celtic milieu (M. SZABÓ 1975: 151), and in appearance are closer to the pseudo-filigree discs on one type of Middle La Tène fibula (M. SZABÓ 1975: 147, 148, Pl. I, 2, 3).

In the missing silver part of the find from Szárazd-Regöly, which was attributed to the same atelier as the golden part of the hoard (M. SZABÓ 1975: 152, 153, Fig. 7), and on which the granulation is also somewhat disorganized, the anthropomorphic decoration of a small mask is supplemented with horizontal and perpendicular double filigree edges, and on these are soldered individual granules placed in a wire frame, identical to those of the little handles on nos. 5 – 7 (Fig. 3a). The Szárazd-Regöly hoard is considered to have been manufactured in the 2nd century BC or somewhat earlier, and deposited in the 1st century BC, and the atelier in which it was made was hypothetically located in the area of the Scordisci or in southern Transdanubia (M. SZABÓ 1975: 155; R. and V. MEGAW 1996: 166). Through the small mask, as a Celtic decorative motif, the find is also considered related to the cult vessel from Gundestrup (M. SZABÓ 1975: 155, Pl. IX, 4, 5), which in recent interpretations has been defined as a product created around 100 BC and attributed to the Scordisci from the section of the region where they mixed with the Thracian Triballi (F. KAUL 1991: 538).³¹

In Thracian filigree jewellery, the rosettes appear as a decorative element only in the most widespread, unified flat version of soldering wire threads onto a background in the form of petals (THRAKER 1979: 91, no. 161, 152, no. 296 etc.), identical to those in other jewellery productions, while the relief rosettes with a granule on the top, as on no. 1, and nos. 5 – 7, do not otherwise appear. Geometric motifs dominate the granulated pieces of jewellery from the Thracian region, most often in the form of flat triangular fields filled with grains (THRAKER 1979: 89, 90, 96, 175, no. 158, no. 159, no. 174, no. 349) or in the form of granulated pyramids (THRAKER 1979: 96, 97, no. 174; G. KITOV 2003: 12, Fig. 7).

A close or the closest analogy of motifs and elements is displayed only on Thracian earrings: vertical dividing rows of granules from golden examples from Duvanli near Plovdiv from the

---

²⁹ There is no visible point of reference to the Etruscan manner of tracing contours or filling the decorative surface (G. NESTLER – E. FORMIGLI 1994: 28, 32, nos. 19, 25), nor to the Greek (F. H. MARSHALL 1911: 105, Pl. XIV, 1240; G. BECATTI 1955: 197, Pl. CIII, 391), or more modest Roman manner of arranging granules (G. BECATTI 1955: 213, 214, Pl. CXLIV, 505, 506), nor to the granulated jewellery of the Illyrian region (BLAGO 1975: 20, nos. 11, 13) or even the Nordic region (E. NYLÉN 1970, Pl. 26, 2, 3, 5), all of the latter having derived from the filigree arts of the Etruscans and Greeks.

³⁰ Apparently similar rosettes also appear among Germanic jewellery, but this was not actually granulation, but rather tiny silver bars, or pseudo-filigree work: J. WERNER 1941: 23 – 27, Fig. 5, Pl. 11 – Pl. 13.

³¹ In the earlier publications of this vessel, with dates assigned to the 2nd century BC, where attention was directed to the religious syncretism of the depictions and other important aspects (J. J. HATT 1980: 68, 284), and also in the more recent analyses, the vegetative decoration of a Dionysian character remained secondary, with ivy leaves produced in a manner that might speak in support of the presence of a certain Illyrian component.

5th century BC (THRAKER 1979: 96, 97, no. 173), and triple tall wire cones, located between two discs, on gold earrings from Botevgrad and Vidbol, dated to the 2nd and 3rd centuries AD (L. RUSEVA-SLOKOSKA 1991: 115, Cat. No. 28, Cat. No. 29), fully correspond to the same details on nos. 3 and 4, while the edges of the discs were of spirally twisted wire, made in an identical manner as the relief rosettes on examples no. 1, no. 2, and nos. 5 – 7.

The cited analogies, based on Hungarian and Bulgarian finds, do not imply a possibility of attributing this group to one of two ethnos, rather – in terms of the manner of creating the filigree – merely the possibility of identifying the achievements in execution and to some extent style resulting from traditions within the Thracian-Celtic production circle a.

The fact is well known that filigree was unknown to the Celts and that the eastern Celts owed that technique to their Thracian-Illyrian surroundings, and that a Thracian component was certainly integrated into their goldsmithing (V. KRUTA 1991: 202; O. H. FREY – M. SZABÓ 1991: 483).

Specimens nos. 1 – 7, nos. 10 – 18, and in part no. 19, should be considered Thracian-Celtic products, created in the 1st century BC in some Balkan lower Danubian workshop. The most suitable region to place such workshops, whose ability to accumulate very varied influences set up the basis for the development of mixed forms, would be the northwest part of present-day Bulgaria. This area was subject to long-term processes of the mingling of ethnic groups with diverse affinities and predispositions in artistic and craft production, inspired by the Greek tradition. At the same time, this was also the area of the lengthy contacts and coexistence between the Scordisci and the Triballi in the 1st century BC, where in the middle or towards the end of the same century, conditions existed for the creation of this filigree group. Such a classification is further supported by the partial gilding, characteristic for Thracian-Dacian toreutics in the period from the 4th to the 1st centuries BC,[32] which was also used to coat the figural depictions on the Gundestrup cauldron. The same is true for the terminals and domed buttons on the chain necklace no. 19, while the chain itself could perhaps be considered a Greek product.[33]

The results of the analysis of the craftsmanship have offered a basis for limiting the boundaries of the cultural identity of the filigree group and its location in the Thracian region, but did not contribute to deciphering the enigma of the purpose of specimen nos. 3 – 7.

The second group, forged with engraved decoration, which includes pendants nos. 8 and 9, and the torcs and bracelets nos. 20 – 41 (Fig. 32), as well as the clasps on the chain necklace no. 19 (Fig. 6b), contains heterogeneous forms and reflects a more complicated image of Thracian-Dacian-Illyrian influences, along with Celtic influence, which is manifested by the torcs themselves as an originally Celtic object.

Various elements of the examples of this forged group are so mixed that it is almost impossible to distinguish the original ethnic characteristics. The most striking depictions on them are of snakes, whose cult was known in the Balkans from as early as the Neolithic period, but in the course of time the snake came to lose its symbolic meaning and remained utilized merely as a decoration.

The torcs and bracelets with snake protomes nos. 20 – 22 and nos. 32 – 37 feature stylized elements based on the autochthonous formula – seemingly – of a predominant Illyrian artistic expression, which is perhaps to some extent explainable by the popularity and special role of the snake, as the totemic animal of certain Illyrian groups.[34]

The torcs with geometric decoration consisting of circles, triangles, rhombs, and various impressed

---

[32] This gilding is present in the form of a lemon-coloured coating not merely on vessels, rhytons, and phalerae, but also torcs and bracelets from Thraco-Dacian hoards: D. POPESCU 1940: 196; 1948: 35, 36, Fig. 1, 2, 3, Fig. 5; 1958: 162 - 170, Figs. 4 -12; J. DÖRIG 1987: 9, 10, Pl. 2 - 10; THRAKER 1979: 140 - 142, 193 - 195, nos. 268, 269, 272, 274, 278, 279, 390 - 392; DACI 1997: 180, 182, 196, 197, 341, nos. 130, 134, 135 - 139, 177, 178, 786), but it can also be found on the jewellery of the Iberian Celts (CELTI 1991: 399, 402).

[33] Because of the quite abundant presence of the woven chains in local Balkan milieus and their high quality of workmanship, with centuries of unchanged quality, the impression is that already woven chains arrived from some specialized – most probably Greek – workshop in local ateliers, where they were cut and finished off by the addition of clamp ends and clasps.

[34] The tradition of totemism among the southern Illyrians was quite strong: the name of the mythic hero Illyrius, the son of Cadmus and Harmonia, was closely related to the snake, whose power he had adopted (and the great snake of the Indo-European Hittites bore a name with the same root): A. STIPČEVIĆ 1974: 19, 182, 183.

rows, nos. 23 – 29, are chronologically and culturally undeterminable because of the decoration based on an inclination to geometric design inherited from the accumulation of earlier traditions if the central Balkan region,[35] which evolved into a widely accepted universal element, even present on jewellery from the Roman period.

A more distinct fit with Thracian traditions is displayed by pendants no. 8 and no. 9, while a complete concordance with Thracian forms was shown by torcs nos. 30 and 31.

A conservative consistency of the early linear motifs is otherwise well illustrated by the silver phalerae from the vicinity of Krumovgrad in southern Bulgaria dated to the 2nd century AD (THRAKER 1979: 210, 212, nos. 428 - 431), with depictions of the Giants, Hercules, and Athena, which on the wide flat edge had engraved segmented decoration, with a net-like motif of hatched incisions inside it exhibiting a startling similarity to no. 22.

The smooth bracelets nos. 38 – 41 (Fig. 23 a, b and 24) with traces of forging not removed fit best into a Dacian context, and their craftsmanship exhibits the same careless approach devoid of any need for perfection that characterizes all the objects in this second group, with the exception of the more carefully worked pendants no. 8 and no. 9, and bracelet no. 32 with a slightly different nuance of the silver.

The specimens from this group give the impression of being the products of one or more workshops with recognizable traits. The spirally twisted circlets of the torcs are not made from wire, but from thick four-edged bars, with each of the four sides hollowed by shallow or deep lengthwise grooves: depending on the sharpness of the edges and the borders of the grooves on the bars or their bluntness or roundedness, the necklaces can give the impression of multi-banded twisted wires of angled or circular section. Along with this, in a manner of speaking, "pseudo" spiral twisting, the craftsmanship is also characterized by a fairly coarse level of production, with a careless rendition and lack of finishing.

The cited workshop characteristics are similar to those noted for finds from Dacian hoards, as "technically primitive with a barbarous appearance" (D. POPESCU 1940: 194). With the exception of pendants no. 8 and no. 9, which are dated earlier, this group of objects made by forging represents the youngest part of the hoard, which would probably correspond chronologically to the quite late 1st century AD.

The third group consists of pendants nos. 42 – 46 (Fig. 30), cut from thin sheet metal with a design chased through a stencil. This set should be considered an artefact directly based on the original form of an eastern Celtic predecessor,[36] from which later forms of pendants were also derived for horse equipment. This set represents a Celtic-Thracian version with an elementary lunar-solar decoration.

The arguments for such a classification are based on much older comparative examples with clearly dual elements incorporated into their ornamentation. The Thracian component on the pendants of the group made in an embossed technique was present as a uniform solar motif in the form of a domed protrusion encircled by a ring-shaped row of beads, which in better worked forms can be found in the Thracian region as early as the 5th century BC on the golden pectorals from a male grave at Duvanli near Plovdiv, attributed to the local workshops in the area (THRAKER 1979: 28, 96, 97, no. 175 and 176). Although segments of ribbed rows can also be seen on some Thracian pectorals (THRAKER 1979: 107, no. 195), the borders on the embossed group can evidently be attributed to Celtic components: they are equivalent to borders composed of relief smooth folds and bead-like rows, which enclose the masks of the early Celtic style on golden embossed decorative sheet-metal elements discovered in the Rhine Valley and also dated to the 5th century BC (CELTI 1991: 136, 162; TRIER 1991: 13, Fig. 5; R. and V. MEGAW 1996: 70, Fig. 74); this is also clearly reflected in the teardrop-shaped ends of the arms, formed in a purely Celtic style.

---

[35] This can be traced from the Early and Late Iron Ages onwards in the Balkan region (ILIRI I DAČANI 1971: 85, 86, 8 – 10; M. GARAŠANIN 1973, Pl. 113; J. TODOROVIĆ 1974: 80, no. 57; T. ARNĂUT – R. URSU NANIU 1996: 111, Pl. XXXVII, 5, Pl. XXXIX, 2 – 4), but also outside it (CELTI 1991: 154; T. GRASSELT 1999: 77, Fig. 20).

[36] Which could perhaps be attributed to that branch of the eastern Celts who in the 3rd century founded the kingdom of Tylis (or Tyle), somewhere in the vicinity of the Balkan Mountains (Haemus) in Thrace: O. H. FREY – M. SZABÓ 1991: 481; R. and V. MEGAW 1996: 123.

The wire loops for attachment should also be mentioned here, formed in a manner quite typical for local Dacian and Thracian production (ILIRI I DAČANI 1971: 161, D 158; DACI 1997: 240, no. 463).

The entire embossed decoration featuring quite high relief was carried out using instruments from the rear side. The pendants were formed routinely, the decoration required great experience, but considering the lapses, the total impression would indicate a craftsmanship almost at the level of the previous group. The sheet metal set of no. 42 – no. 46 was contemporary to the filigree group of objects from the hoard, with which they share the same cultural context and perhaps also the same workshop provenience. The production of the set can be attributed to the same workshop circle that also manufactured identical pendants for a belt from Vidin (I. ŠOPOVA 2004: 345, no. 352h).

In summary it can be concluded that the hoard, which can be dated to a relative framework of the 1st century BC – 1st century AD, contains objects with mixed elements, subject to various influences, the most evident being Thracian and Celtic, as equal factors in formation, along with an intrinsic Greek background component. The hoard has a partial source in the culture of the late La Tène, but extends chronologically into the Roman period, when Illyrians, Thracian, and Celts no longer existed per se,[37] and it might indicate an autochthonous segment of the population resistant to the changes that had arrived together with Romanization. The temporal span between the period when the objects from the hoard were created and the period of their deposition extends over almost a century. Although the hoard does not contain so many pure stylistic or craft elements that they would themselves signal the same manufacturer, it is certain that these objects were produced in the Thracian region, in one or more officinae of an advanced technical capacity, with a long experience in making jewellery in various autochthonous forms and with knowledge of classic, but not merely Greek works.

It is difficult to judge the character of the hoard. The most acceptable possibility would seem to indicate a deposit by a wealthy individual from the Thracian population, who in a time of crisis buried objects of permanent material value so as to utilize them again later.[38] Or the hoard was taken to some habitual place once as a votive or sacrificial offering, or was offered at a cult site where ritual ceremonies had taken place several times. However, since no data are available that would strengthen such possibilities, they remain on the level of conjecture.

It is generally considered that Dacian, for example, but also Thracian silver hoards had a ritual character, and perhaps such a trait could also be attributed to this deposit.

It was previously noted that the pendant-axes could have had a cult function, but they are insufficient for characterizing the entire hoard, since such a function for the cylindrical and square containers is uncertain.

The unexpectedly large number of torcs and bracelets would support a ritual character. If the chain with pendants for a horse harness, which can be defined – given the rich decoration – as ceremonial, is considered in the same light, the very possibility exceeds the rank of a hypothesis, as horses played an important role in Thracian spiritual life, both in the religious sphere and in the afterlife.[39] The pendant-axes would also fit well into a ritual context as decoration for horse equipment. However, the filigree specimens no. 3 – no. 7, which barely correspond to the other objects, disrupt every solution, including this one, because of their unclear function. The results of analysis on the basis of their form as well as on the basis of decoration have not contributed to deciphering their enigma, and so far there is no way that these examples can be viewed as either cult or ritual items.

---

[37] Northwest Thrace entered the sphere of Roman policies of conquest in the 1st century BC: D. POPOV 2000: 64; in the same century, with the arrival of the Romans in the Lower Danube basin, the Scordisci disappear from the historical scene: B. JOVANOVIĆ – P. POPOVIĆ 1991: 346.

[38] The jewellery could have been worn for a century and a half (D. POPESCU 1958: 201), and the continuity of the same forms is proven by finds of identical jewellery from silver hoards from the 1st century BC and from the second half of the 1st century AD (D. POPESCU 1940: 187, Fig. 3; ANTIČKO SREBRO 1994: 209, no. 68).

[39] The Thracian male god of unknown name was personified specifically by a horseman: D. POPOV 2000: 103 - 106. The practice of sacrificing horses to accompany the deceased buried under tumuli was retained in Thracian funerary rituals even into the Roman period: D. POPOV 2000: 74.

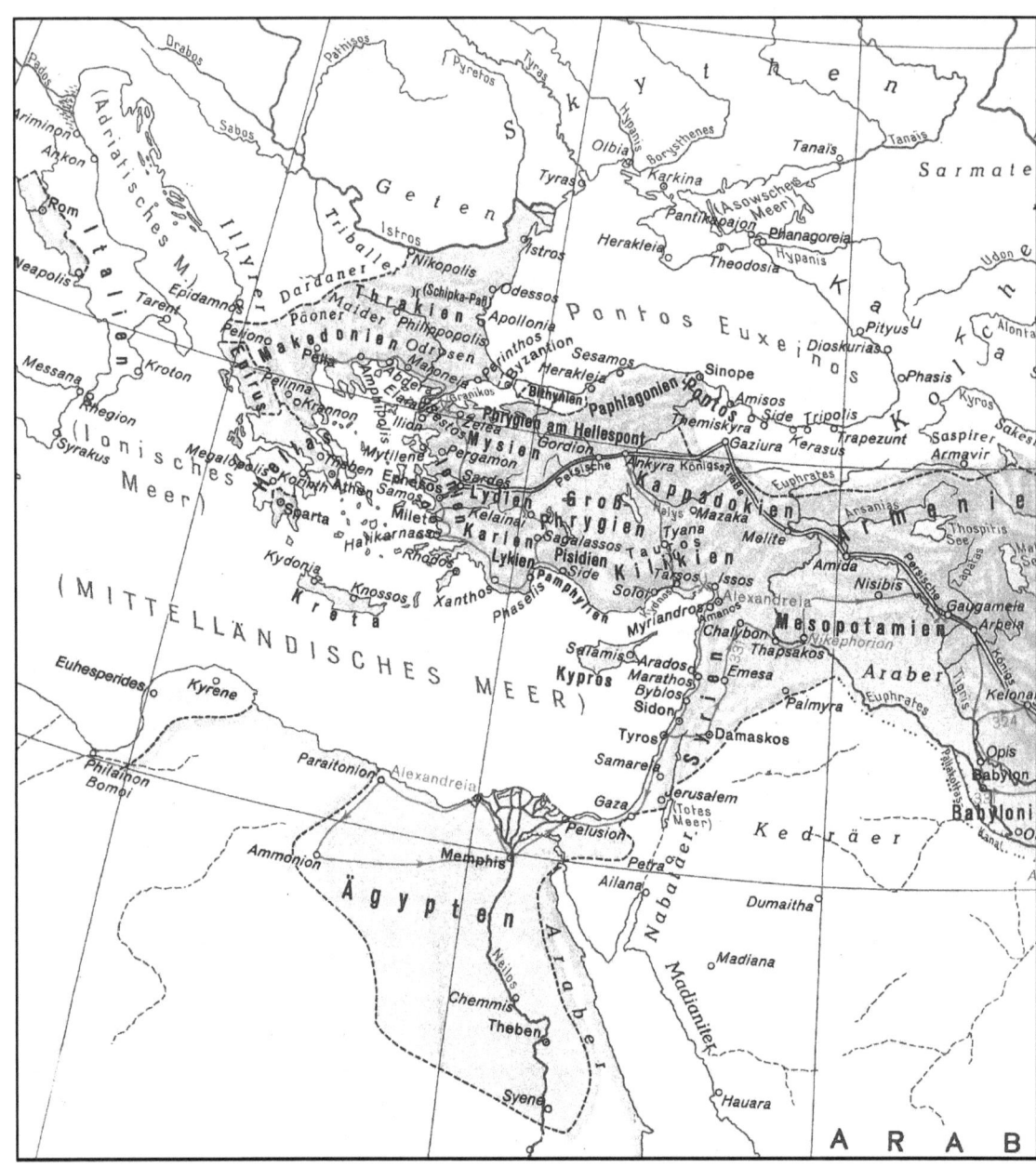

Euroasia in the Time of Alexander the Great

Perhaps to explain them it is necessary to reach far beyond the region of the Balkan Danube basin, into an ambience with a different ethnic identity.

The Thracian tribes inhabited a very large area, and if the Cimmerians were to be included among them,[40] their boundaries would extend in the east beyond the Sea of Azov (R. FLORESCU – G. A. POPESCU 1997: 11), which implies a broad openness to eastern influences. Numerous stylistic similarities have been noted among the artistic and craft products from the Thracian-Dacian-Getaean region, as well as those from the Anatolian-Iranian region, and the Thracian form of expression, along with eastern European elements, also contains elements from the Asian northwest, considered to have been under Iranian (Persian) influence (R. FLORESCU 1997: 88).[41]

The Persian tradition was close to that of the Thracians, especially because of similarities in

---

[40] As considered by some historiographers: Z. VINSKI 1940: 13, 14.
[41] Iranian influence can also be seen in the famous treasure from Panagyurishte, made in the Achaemenid style: D. POPOV 2000: 111.

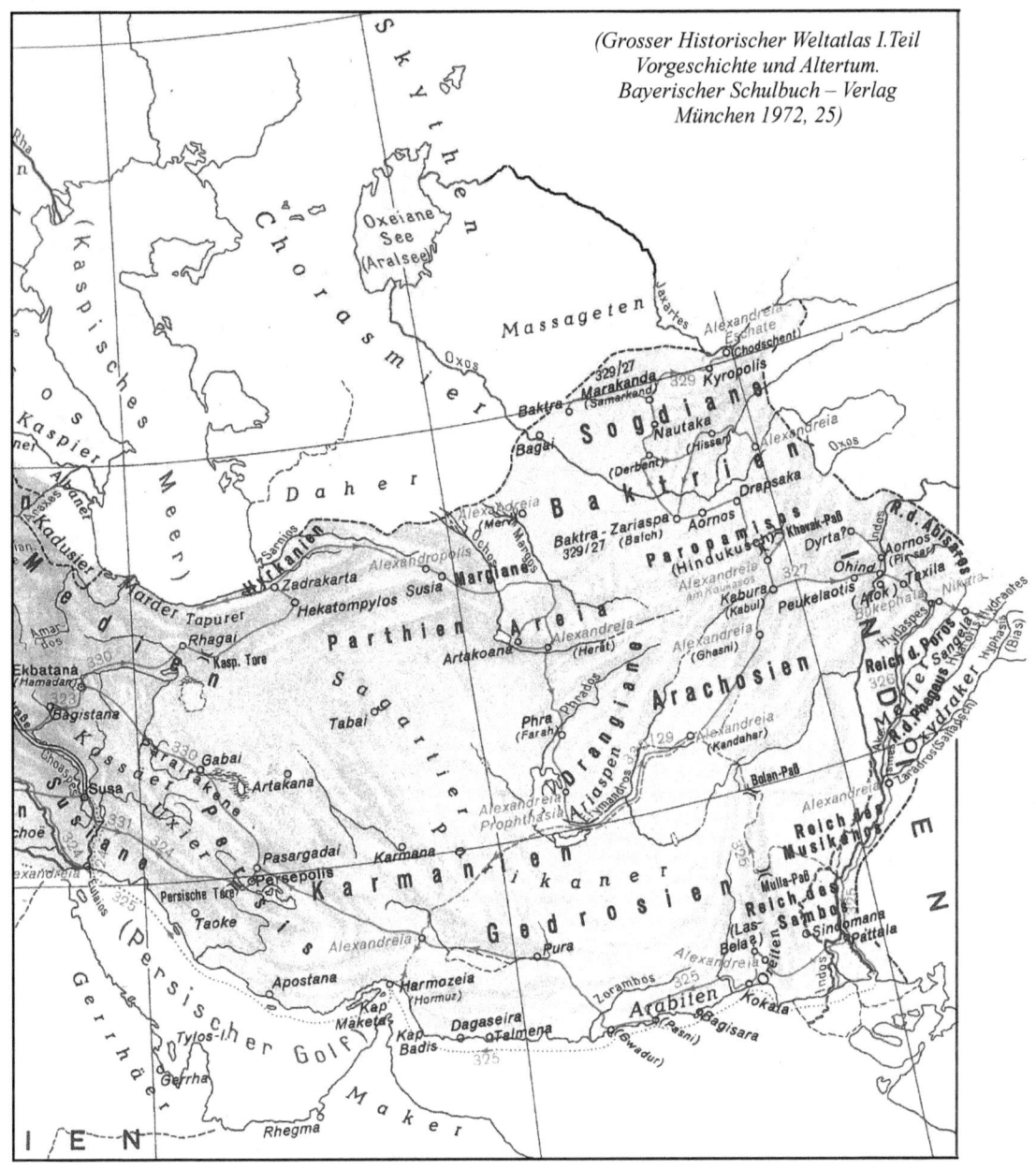

Euroasia in the Time of Alexander the Great (contdinued)

the religious concepts.[42] Achaemenid Persia also played the role of a mediator in the creation of the Scythian animalistic style from southern Russia, significantly present in the Thracian artistic artefacts from the 5th and 4th centuries BC, while in later centuries, such artistic productions were claimed to be a "local variant of a unified phenomenon that extended from Iberia to Bactria" (D. POPOV 2000: 111).

In such a broader geo-historical framework, the possibility of discovering a framework for the placement of forms no. 1 – no. 7 seems more likely.

One direction, probably Near Eastern, is reflected in the previously mentioned drum-shaped pendants, the only purely cylindrical shape noted in the consulted texts, which appeared in a

---

[42] Visual information about their complexity can be noted on the depictions of hybrid goddesses – of strange iconography and hard to fathom semantics – on the silver, partially gilded greaves from princely graves at Vratsa in Bulgaria and Agighiol in Romania from the 5th and 4th centuries BC, which were hesitantly interpreted as products created under Achaemenid influence or as products of Greek workshops that utilized motifs from Persian art: THRAKER 1979: 138, 148, 149, no. 293; DACI 1997: 185, nos. 151 and 152. On the above figure of a female deity on the greave from Vratsa, located in the region of the Thracian Triballi, a torc was depicted with ends in the form of lions, which is considered to be based on a Persian model: O. H. FREY – M. SZABÓ 1991: 479.

Sarmatian context from the late 3rd and the 4th centuries AD, but which certainly had its origins in their Iranian provenience.[43] The pendants come from Vršac in Vojvodina, in appearance like barrels closed on both ends, made of bronze sheet metal and decorated with hammered circular protrusions arranged in spaced rows, while a wire circlet pulled through the wall holds them in a horizontal position. They probably represent part of female attire, and judging from the position on the skeleton where they were found, they could have been attached to a belt or a strap that hung down to the knees (S. BARAČKI 1961: 119, 120, 139, 140, 142; Pl. IV, 10; Pl. VII, 5, 6; Pl. VIII, 5; Pl. IX, 17; Pl. XV, 10, 11).

Another direction leads to Bactria in central Asia, where the finds from wealthy burials with gold inventories included items from female attire where head decorations of caps and diadems particularly stand out, with large pendants hung at the height of temple rings, and the grave goods contained a heart-shaped clasp with granulated edges – the only noted example more or less similar to pendants nos. 1 and 2 (TILLJA-TEPE 1985: 245, no. 45, and the reconstructions on pp. 230, 234, 258). Although they have a completely different form, the cited decorations indicate an insufficient knowledge of numerous attire decorations in antiquity that disappeared without a trace. The presence of a Greek-Bactrian influence in a local variant was otherwise noticeable on other Thracian artefacts, some of which were discovered in this same region of north-western Bulgaria, such as the partially gilded silver phalerae with figural images from the village of Yakimovo, dated to the 1st century BC (A. MILČEV 1973: 3 - 9, Fig. 3, 9).

It is clear that the noted regions, as the possible provenience for the form of nos. 1 – 7, remain at present at a level of speculation, although the previously cited scope of distant eastern influences and their lengthy existence reasonably justify and support such a proposition. The original positioning of similar items would require considerably more detailed knowledge of Transcaucasian, southern Russian, and Asian gold and silver decorative elements.

In terms of the torcs, they fit well into a cult and ritual context, along with bracelets as an accompanying form of jewellery. Even their quantity of over twenty pieces in the hoard would indicate this. Although finds of torcs in the Thracian region on average are not particularly numerous, those depicted on the figural images of male and female deities from the span of the 3rd – 1st centuries BC and the 2nd – 3rd centuries AD are quite common, and it is not rare to find several circlets around the neck of the same figure (A. MILČEV 1973: 8, Fig. 9a, b; THRAKER 1979: 194, 195, no. 391, 222 - 224, no. 464, no. 473; I. ŠOPOVA 2004: 329, no. 302d). The depictions include Sarmatian female deities with birds on their shoulders that have as many as eight torcs around their necks (A. MILČEV 1973: 9; THRAKER 1979: 193, no. 390).

Whether as materially valuable parts of an orientally nuanced lay attire or as parts of some priestly robes, the filigree examples, including nos. 3 – 7, should nonetheless be classified hypothetically in a ritual and cult framework, simply because they originally were attached to other items with such a potential identity.

Further, it should not be disregarded that the hoard comes from a clime that was the central region for the creation of Thracian Orphism, in which the Great Mother Goddess was a central figure. This was a region where numerous personifications of this deity were present, while numerous ancient autochthonous goddesses present under local names, such as a Bendida, Braura, Hipta, Zerynthia, etc., were lost in the Roman period due to syncretisation with the official pantheon. Some light is thrown on their poorly known original iconography, attributes, clothing, jewellery, and so forth by certain images, such as the small bronze sculpture of Cybele from the 6th century BC from Čukarka with interesting, if poorly visible details above the forehead and around the neck (E. PENKOVA 2004: 204), or the much later bronze relief with an archaic bust of Cybele from the 2nd century AD from Razgrad with three torcs around the neck and with a tall khalatos on the head, with ribbons hanging down on both sides with attached bells and drums (K. MAJEWSKI 1969: 187, Fig. 161; I. ŠOPOVA 2004: 329, no. 302c). Although in the last case, these were the standard attributes of the Great Goddess, from their dimensions and positions a possible likelihood can be noted of the existence of other requisites and jewellery in local iconographies.

---

[43] Persian roots were more emphasized among the Sarmatians than their compatriots the Scythians: Z. VINSKI 1940: 17. The Sarmatians were also the successive neighbours of the Dacians to the northeast: R. FLORESCU – G. A. POPESCU 1997: 12.

Bulgarian Archaeological Sites
(THRAKER, 19)

In conclusion, it is necessary to compare the hoard with other such published hoard finds from Bulgaria.

Among the known finds of treasures with torcs from the Thracian region, such as Čauševo, Nikolaevo, Bazaurt, Ratiaria (L. RUSEVA-SLOKOSKA 1991: 210 - 212), the inventory of the discussed deposit is closest to the partly published and previously cited silver hoard found by the city of Vidin (Roman Bononia), dated to the 1st cent. BC – 1st cent. AD, which was likewise placed in a clay vessel (I. ŠOPOVA 2004: 344, 345, no. 352). Both hoards display a surprising similarity, not merely in the composition of the objects they contain, but also the quantities of examples of individual types. Their mutual characteristics involve a corresponding number of torcs and bracelets, although the forms either cannot be directly compared or are different, the presence of identical woven chains, and primarily the appearance of identical lunular pendants in equal numbers. The hoard from Vidin is essential for solving various problems related to the hoard discussed here, and its more detailed publication would certainly offer or supplement answers to essential questions about the cultural, specific geographic, and workshop origins, as well as those about the purpose – the profane, ritual, or cult character – of both hoards.

POSTSCRIPTUM

With the publication of this silver hoard from the Lower Danube valley, the final aim has been fulfilled of removing it from anonymity and incorporating it into the memory of civilization.

However, the finds that were the very reason for this study once again direct attention to the Balkans, as a controversial region in the contemporary understanding of the inveterate stereotype. Like all the previous items, the objects presented here represent a diminutive contribution to liberating the Balkans from their label with a negative connotation, signalling the need for their reaffirmation. The Balkans are a border region in the most positive sense of a detachment from exposure to complete assimilation, but in return represent an epicentre for the intensive intermingling of western and eastern cultures. The distance of its position allowed the Balkan region to avoid the seductive power of Greek civilization, primarily adopting universal Hellenistic achievements, and to evade the unifying standards of Roman culture. This was a place of alternative development, beyond the main favoured directions, which formed one of the most interesting cultures within the boundaries of the Graeco-Roman world. Stemming from hybrid ethnic foundations, with identities submerged into a distinctive mixture, this culture manifests the influences of widespread Euro-Asian circulation. Devoid of the supreme perfectionism necessary for classical evaluation, it displays a specific charm and an exceptional vitality in the transformation, modification, and adaptation of forms, creating mixed forms with a stamp of originality. The high quality of its products reflect a potential of cosmopolitan proportions, which to some extent represents a pledge for the future, further opening creative perspectives spanning the almost inexhaustible resources of these same eternal Balkans.

Zagreb April, 15 2010

ABBREVIATIONS

Alba Regia   Annales Musei Stephani Regis (Székesfehérvár)

Arheologija Organ na Arheologičeskija Institut i Muzej pri Bulgarska Akademija na naukite (Sofija)

AVe   Arheološki vestnik. Slovenska Akademija znanosti in umetnosti. Razred za zgodovinske i družbene vede - Sekcija za arheologijo (Ljubljana)

BAR IntSer British Archaeological Reports, International Series (Oxford)

Britannia A Journal of Romano-British and Kindred studies (London)

Dacia Revue d'archéologie et d'histoire ancienne. Académie de la République populaire roumaine (Bucarest)

DissArchGand Dissertationes Archaeologicae Gandenses (Brugge)

DissMonB   Dissertationes et Monographiae. Savez Arheoloških društava Jugoslavije (Beograd)

DissPann Dissertationes Pannonicae (Budapest)

Germania   Korrespondenzblatt der Römisch-Germanischen Kommission des Deutschen Archäologischen Instituts (Frankfurt)

GZM Glasnik Zemaljskog muzeja BiH (Sarajevo)

JRGZ Jahrbuch des Römisch-Germanischen Zentralmuseums Mainz (Mainz)

KärntMussch   Kärntner Museumsschriften. Archäologische Forschungen zu den Grabungen auf dem Magdalensberg (Klagenfurt)

KatMon Katalogi in monografije. Narodni muzej Slovenije (Ljubljana)

KleiSchriSD Kleine Schriften zu Kenntnis der römischen Besetzungsgeschichte Süwestdeutschland (Stuttgart)

Latomus Revue d'études latines (Bruxelles)

RdA   Rivista di Archeologia (Roma)

RömGermFor   Römisch Germanische Forschungen (Berlin)

RVM Rad Vojvođanskih muzeja (Novi Sad)

SaalbJb Saalburg Jahrbuch. Bericht des Saalburgmuseums (Frankfurt/Berlin)

SchrifRheinT   Schriftenreihe des Rheinischen Landesmuseums Trier (Trier)

WMBH Wissenschaftlische Mitteilungen aus Bosnia und Herzegowina. Bosnisch-Herzegowinisches Landesmuseum Sarajevo (Wien)

BIBLIOGRAPHY

ANTIČKO SREBRO:
1994. Antičko srebro u Srbiji. Antique Silver from Serbia – exhibition catalogue (I. Popović), Beograd.
ARNĂUT T. – URSU NANIU R.:
1996. Vestigii Getice din a doua epocă a fierului în interfluviul Pruto-Nistrean (Vestiges Gétiques de la seconde epoque du fer dans l'interfleuve Pruto-Nistreen), Academia Română – Filiala IAŞI Institutul da arheologie IAŞI, Bucarest.
BARAČKI S.:
1961. Sarmatski nalazi iz Vršca, RVM 10., 117-142.
BECATTI G.:
1955. Oreficerie antiche dalle minoiche alle barbariche, Roma.
BISHOP M. C.:
1987. The Evolution of Certain Features. Roman Military Equipment - Accoutrements of War - Proceedings of the Third Roman Military Equipment Seminar (ed. by M. Dowson), BAR IntSer 336, 109-139.
1988. Cavalry Equipment of the Roman Army in the First Century A.D. Military Equipment and the Identity of Roman Soldiers - Proceedings of the Fourth Roman Military Equipment Conference (ed. by J. C. Coulston), BAR IntSer 394, 67-339.
BLAGO:
Grčko-ilirsko blago – katalog izložbe (V. Kondić), Narodni muzej u Beogradu, Beograd 1975.
BOGNÁR KUTZIÁN I.:
1975. Some New Early La Tène Finds in the Northern Danube Basin, Alba Regia XIV, 35-46.
BÖHME A.:
1974. Schmuck der römischen Frau, KleiSchriSD 11.
BULLINGER H.:
1969. Spätantike Gürtelbeschläge-Typen, Herstellung, Trageweise und Datierung, DissArchGand XII.
CANTACUZINO G.:
1948. Antiquités inédites de Olténie, Dacia XI – XII (1945 – 1947), 313-322.
CELTI:
1991. I Celti – katalog izložbe (S. Moscati et al.), Milano.
CHŁODNICKI M.:
1996. Skarby Muzeum Archeologicznego w Poznaniu-Historia ich pozyskania zaginięcia i odzyskania. Die Schätze des Archäologischen Museums zu Poznań- Erworben-verloren-wiedergefunden, Poznań.
CICHORIUS C.:
1896 - 1900. Die Reliefs der Traianssäule-Herausgegeben und historisch Erklärt Gedruckt mit Unterstützung des Königlich Sächsischen Ministeriums des Cultur und Öffentlichen Unterrichts. Erste Tafelband-Die Reliefs des Ersten Dakischen Krieges (Tafel 1-57), Zweiter Tafelband-Die Reliefs des Zweiten Dakischen Krieges (Tafel 58-113), Berlin.
CRIŞAN I. H.:
1959. Les trésors d'Aţel et les relations balkano-danubiens, Dacia III, 353-367.
CROAZIA:
1993. Arte e cultura in Croazia - Collezioni del Museo Archeologico di Zagabria – exhibition catalogue (Ed. A. Rendić Miočević), Torino.
ČREMOŠNIK I.:
1963. Nošnja na rimskim spomenicima u Bosni i Hercegovini, GZM XVIII, 103-121.
1964. Die einheimliche Tracht Noricums, Pannoniens und Illyriens und ihre Vorbilder, Latomus 23.
DACI:

1997. I Daci – exhibition catalogue (G. A. Popescu), Milano.
DAIRE M. Y.:
1991. L'Armorica, in: CELTI, 237-250.
DEDEOĞLU J. (ÖZ):
1993. Izmir Archaeological Museum, Istanbul.
DEIMEL M.:
1987. Die Bronzekleinfunde vom Magdalensberg, KärnMussch 71.
DÖRIG J.:
1987. Les trésors d'orfèvrerie thrace, RdA Suppl. 3.
DUMITRESCU V.:
1968. La nécropole tumulaire du premier âge du fer de Basarabi (Dép. de Dolj, Olténie), Dacia XII, 177-260.
EGG M. – PARE C.:
1995. Die Metallzeiten in Europa und im Vorderen Orient - Die Abteilung Vorgeschichte im Römisch-Germanischen Zentralmuseum, Römisch-Germanisches Zentralmuseum-Forschungsinstitut für Vor-und Frügeschichte, Mainz.
ELUÈRE C.:
1991. L'oro, in: CELTI, 349-355.
ETTLINGER E.:
1975. Die römische Fibeln in der Schweiz, Hadbuch der Schweiz zur Römer- und Merowingerzeit, Bern.
FLORESCU R.:
1997. L'arte dei Daci, in: DACI, 79-89.
FLORESCU R. – POPESCU G. A.:
1997. Lo stato e la civiltà dei Daci, in: DACI, 11-20.
FRANZ L.:
1940. Ein Tierkopfring aus Armenien, Hoffillerov zbornik-Serta Hoffilleriana, Zagreb, 83-85.
FREY O. H. – SZABÓ M.:
1991. I Celti nell'area balcanica, in: CELTI, 478-484.
GARAŠANIN M.:
1973. Praistorija Srbije II - gvozdeno doba, Beograd.
GIOIELLI:
Gioielli e ornamenti dagli Egizi all'Alto Medioevo – exhibition catalogue (P. Zamarchi Grassi), Museo Archeologico di Arezzo, Arezzo 1988.
GOSPODARI SREBRA:
Gospodari srebra - Gvozdeno doba na tlu Srbije. Masters of Silver - The Iron Age in Serbia – exhibition catalogue (M. Vukmanović – P. Medović), Narodni muzej u Beogradu/National Museum, Beograd 1990.
GRASSELT T.:
1999. Die späthallstattzeitlichen Gräber von Henfstädt-Strick, Lkr. Hildburghausen, Alt-Thüringen-Jahresschrift des Thüringischen Landesamtes für Archäologische Denkmalpflege 33, Weimar/Stuttgart.
GSCHWANTLER K.:
1999. Die Anhänger der Kette und ihre Deutung, in: Barbarenschmuck und Römergold – Der Schatz von Szilágysomlyó – exhibition catalogue (W. Seipel), Kunsthistorisches Museum Wien, Wien, 63-79.
GUŠTIN M.:
1991. Posočje in der jüngeren Eisenzeit. Posočje v mlajši železni dobi, KatMon 27.
HATT J. J.:
1980. Eine Interpretation der Bilder und Szenen auf dem Silberkessel von Gundestrup, in: Die Kelten in Mitteleuropa – exhibition catalogue (L. Pauli), Salzburg, 68-75.
ILAKOVAC B.:
1976. Portretna medalja iz Burnuma, AVes XXV, 158-164.
ILIRI I DAČANI:
Iliri i Dačani. The Illyrians and Dacians – exhibition catalogue (D. Garašanin et al.), Narodni muzej u Beogradu/National Museum, Beograd 1971.
IŞIK BINGÖL F. R.:
1999. Ancient Jewellery, Museum of Anatolian Civilisations, Ankara.
JENKINS I.:

1985. A Group of Silvered-Bronze Horse-Trappings from Xanten (Castra Vetera), Britannia XVI, 141-164.
JOVANOVIĆ A.:
1978. Nakit u rimskoj Dardaniji, DissMonB XXI.
JOVANOVIĆ B. – POPOVIĆ P.:
1991. Gli Scordisci, in: CELTI, 337-347.
JUNKELMANN M.:
1986. Die Legionen des Augustus-Kulturgeschichte der Antiken Welt 33, Mainz.
KITOV G.:
2003. The Valley of the Thracian Rulers. Slavena, Varna.
2003/1: Thracian Cult Center near Starosel. Slavena, Varna.
KONOVA L.:
2004. Königsstädte, Residenzen, Tempel und Siedlungen im vorrömischen Thrakien, in: THRAKER I, 134-141.
2004/1. Thrakisch-griechische Synthesen, in: THRAKER I, 278-285.
KAUL F.:
1991. Il calderone di Gundestrup, in: CELTI, 538.
KRUTA V.:
1991. I Celti della prima espansione storica (IV secolo a.C.), in: CELTI, 195-213.
LAWSON A. K.:
1982. Studien zum Römischen Pferdegeschirr, JRGZ 25 (1978), 131-160.
MAGIE:
Die Magie des Goldes-Antike Schätze aus Italien – exhibition catalogue (W. Seipel), Kunsthistorisches Museum Wien, Wien 1996.
MAJEWSKI K.:
1969. Kultura Rzymska w Bułgarii, Ossolineum. Zaklad narodowy imenia Ossolinskich. Wydawnictwo polskej Akademii Nauk, Wroclaw-Warszawa-Kraków.
MAJNARIĆ PANDŽIĆ N.:
1970. Keltsko-latenska kultura u Slavoniji i Srijemu, Gradski muzej u Vinkovcima, Vinkovci.
MANO ZISI Đ.:
1957. Nalaz iz Tekije. Les trouvailles de Tekiya, Narodni muzej u Beogradu – Antika II, Beograd.
MARSHALL F. H.:
1911. Catalogue of Jewellery Greek, Etruscan and Roman in the Department of Antiquities, British Museum, London.
MEGAW R. and V.:
1996. Celtic Art – From its Beginnings to the Book of Kells, London.
MEGAW J. V. S. – MEGAW M. R. – NEUGEBAUER J. W.:
1997. Kleine Mitteilungen, Germania 75, 717-735.
MILČEV A.:
1973. Novootkrito srebrno trakijsko skrovišče ot s. Jakimovo III, Mihajlovgradsko, Arheologija XV/1, 1-14.
MILLER S. G.:
1979. Two Groups of Thessalian Gold, Classical Studies, University of California Publications 18, University of California Press, Berkeley/Los Angeles/London.
MINNS E. H.:
1965. Scythians and Greeks - A Survey of Ancient History and Archaeology on the North Coast of the Euxine from Danube to the Caucasus I, II, New York.
MOGA M.:
1948. Dépôt de Guruslău (Département de Sălaj), Dacia XI – XII (1945 – 1947), 257-264.
NESTLER G. – FORMIGLI E.:
1994. Granulazione etrusca - Un'antica tecnica orafa, Siena.
NICOLĂECSU PLOPŞOR C. S.:
1948. Antiquités celtiques en Olténie, Dacia XI – XII (1945 – 1947), 17-34.
NYLÉN E.:
1970. Die älteste Goldschmiedekunst der Nordischen Eisenzeit und ihr Ursprung, JRGZ 15 (1968), 75-94.
PATCH C.:
1909. Archäologisch-epigraphische Untersuchungen zur Geschichte der römischen Provinz Dalmatien, WMBH XI.

PATEK E.:
1942. Verbreitung und Herkunft der römischen Fibeltypen von Pannonien, DissPann II/19.
PENKOVA E.:
2004. Das mythische und das legendäre Thrakien, in: THRAKER I, 203-213.
PETROVIĆ J.:
1941. Ilirsko-rimsko blago iz Šabca, GZM 1941, 11-23.
POPESCU D.:
1940. Objets de parure géto-daces en argent, Dacia VII – VIII (1937 – 1940), 183-202.
1948. Nouveaux trésors géto-daces en argent-Trésor de Herăstrău, Dacia XI – XII (1945 – 1946), 35-70.
1958. Le trésor dace de Sîncrăieni, Dacia II, 157-206.
POPOV D.:
2000. Tračka civilizacija – Tračani-društvo, politika, kultura, Beograd.
POPOVIĆ LJ. B.:
1994. Antička grčka zbirka. Collection of Greek Antiquities, Narodni muzej u Beogradu-Antika VII/National Museum in Belgrade-Antiquity VII, Beograd.
PRAISTORIJA:
Praistorija Jugoslavenskih Zemalja V - željezno doba (A. Benac et al.), ANU BiH -Centar za balkanološka ispitivanja, Sarajevo 1987.
PREDA C.:
1961. Archaeological discoveries in the Greek cemetery of Callatis-Mangalia (IVth - IIIrd centuries before our era), Dacia V, 276-303.
RAŠAJSKI R.:
1961. Dačka srebrna ostava iz Kovina, RVM 10, 7-22.
REINACH S.:
1894. Antiqutés nationales. Description raisonné du Musée du Saint-Germain-en-Laye – Bronzes figurés de la Gaule Romaine, Paris.
ROSTOVCEV M.:
1974. Istorija starog sveta - Grčka i Rim, Subotica.
ROUALET P.:
1991. La "facies marniana" della Campagne, in: CELTI, 147-154.
RUSEVA-SLOKOSKA L.:
1991. Roman Jewellery. A Collection of the National Archaeological Museum Sofia, Sofia.
STIERLIN H.:
2006. Splendeurs de l'Empire Perse. Paris
STIPČEVIĆ A.:
1974. Iliri - povijest, život, kultura, Zagreb.
SZABÓ M.:
1975. Sur la question du filigrane dans l'art des Celtes Orientaux, Alba Regia XIV, 147-165.
1991. Il mercenariato, in: CELTI, 333-336.
ŠOPOVA I.:
2004. Thracia Christiana, in: THRAKER I, 322-327-
THRAKER:
Gold der Thraker-Archäologische Schätze aus Bulgarien – exhibition catalogue (I. Wenedikov – I. Marasow), Mainz 1979.
THRAKER I:
Die Thraker. Das goldene Reich des Orpheus – exhibition catalogue (J.Wenzel et al.), Bonn 2004.
TILLJA TEPE:
Baktrisches Gold aus den Ausgrabungen der Nekropole von Tillja Tepe in Nordafganistan, Institut für Archäologie der Akademie der Wissenschaften der Ud SSR, Moskau – National Museum der Demokratischen Republik Afganistans, Kabul, Leningrad 1985.
TODOROVIĆ J.:
1968. Kelti u jugoistočnoj Evropi. Die Kelten in Süd-Ost Europa, Dissertationes VII, Muzej grada Beograda, Beograd.
1974. Skordisci - Istorija i kultura. The Skordisci - History and Culture, Institut za izučavanje istorije Vojvodine – Savez arheoloških društava Jugoslavije, Novi Sad/Beograd.
TRÉSORS:
Trésors des Empereurs d'Autriche - Les collections d'antiquités grecques et romaines du Kunsthistorisches Museum, Vienne – exhibition catalogue (A. Bernhard Walcher et al.), Musée

de la civilisation, Québec 1994.
TRIER:
Das Rheinische Landesmuseum Trier – guide (L. Schwinden et al.), SchrifRheinT 5, 1991.
TROY
The Treasure of Troy. H. Schliemann's Excavations – exhibition catalogue (V.Tolstikov - M.Treister), Moskva 1996.
URLEB M.:
1974. Križna gora pri Ložu - Halštatska nekropola. Hallstattzeitlisches Gräberfeld Križna gora, KatMon 11.
1975. Halštatska nekropola na Križni gori pri Ložu, AVes XXIV (1973), 507-514.
VINSKI Z.:
1940. Uz problematiku starog Irana i Kavkaza s osvrtom na podrijetlo Anta i Bijelih Hrvata (posvećeno dr. C. Patch-u o 75-godišnjici života), Zagreb.
WERNER J.:
1941. Die Beiden Zierscheiben des Thorsberger Moorfundes-Ein Beitrag zu Frühgermanischen Kunst- und Religionsgeschichte, RömGermFor 16.
1953. Keltisches Pferdegeschirr der Spätlatènezeit, SaalbJb XII, 42-51.

CATALOGUE

1 – 2. A pair of pendants with one face in the form of a figure-eight, with a loop for suspension on the upper edge. Each consists of two thin sheet metal platelets joined by soldering, the front one decorated and the back one smooth and serving as reinforcement. The loops were made from the sheet metal of the upper platelets, while the lower platelets – at the level of the beginning of the loop – had two little horns, which were broken off on the first example. The upper platelets were bordered by a barely visible smooth wire, inside of which a dense row of regular granules was soldered without any spaces between them, which further cover the loop to the final curve, where they were omitted. A perpendicular row of granules extends down the middle of the platelet, cut across at the narrowest point by a horizontal row of somewhat larger granules, which end on the outer edges with three larger grains. The segments of rows of granules soldered alongside the border rows have different lengths, meaning the pendants are not entirely identical. Above and below the horizontal row are symmetrical mirror-image heart-shaped forms made from smooth double-braided wires, onto which – in relatively regular spacing – large granules were soldered, such as can also be found – in an irregular arrangement – within and outside the heart-shaped frame. At the ends and in the middle of the vertical rows are rosettes made of spirally bent smooth wires with a soldered larger central granule. On the surface of the upper platelet, beneath the granulation carried out in silver, a pale yellowish reflection of gilding can be noted.

    Length: 31 mm
    Width: 11 mm
    Depth: 2 mm
    Weight: 1.68 and 1.60 gr
    (Fig. 1 a, b; Pl. I, 1, 2)

3 – 4. A pair of objects in the form of a tiny cylindrical container with a broad banded handle, and filigree decoration located only on the front and lower sides. The small handles are rounded in front, with a sharper angle towards the back, which is flat and merges with the line of the perpendicular walls. The handles and the circular base are soldered onto the walls and the joins are invisible. The container is cut from a sheet metal band, and the perpendicular walls are joined with silver solder on the back. The edge of the opening and the join with the base are bordered with a smooth double wire, carelessly hammered. In the centre of the front half of the container, below the handle, are two perpendicular rows of tiny joined granules of identical size. These dense rows are bordered both inside and out with double-braided smooth wires, also used to make some of the slanted divisions, symmetrically located on both sides of the perpendicular rows. The double wires of the slanted dividers were in general irregularly formed, mostly smooth, but in some places with a braided or bead-like appearance. The dividers form three elongated triangular fields, filled with less dense and irregularly arranged grains, two of which were soldered beyond the edges of the triangular fields. The remaining, rear section of the wall is empty, just like the rear part of the banded handle, while on the latter's front section – along the edges and in the centre – granules were placed with a large space between, soldered onto double, irregularly formed, seemingly smooth wires. A similar gap can be noted on the ring-shaped row of granules located in the middle of the base, encircling an edging wire circle with four small granules, with a small cone rising above them, formed from coils of thin smooth wire, with a larger granule on the tip. The entire surface of the silver sheet metal, inside and out – including the handles – was gilded, which incompletely or partially also covered the rear side, while all of the filigree (granulation) was carried out in silver. The gilding on the front

side appears compact and solid, and even seems untouched on the interior of the container. On both examples, the walls are slightly crumpled in places, including the handle on the first, where there is also insignificant damage in the form of a small hole. On the second example, the original handle was reinforced by a sheet metal band with triangularly cut ends placed below it. The supporting band, probably bronze, is partially covered on the inside (i.e. the side that touches the back of the handle) with a green patina, is elastic, and can be removed from its position.

    Height: 30 mm
    Diam.: 22 mm
    Th. sheet metal: 0.5 mm
    Weight: 3.80 and 4.60 gr (with the supporting band)
    (Fig. 2 a, b; Pl. I, 3, 4)

5 – 7. Three identical examples in the form of a square bag with two narrow banded handles and filigree decoration on the front and lower sides. The handles, which were decorated on the front to the halfway point with a row of granules placed on a circular hammered smooth wire backing framework, were crossed over each other in the centre and the long hammered ends were alternately soldered to the interior of the walls. The smooth surfaced carelessly hammered double silver wire that edges the opening continues along the upper edges of the undecorated lateral and rear walls, while its ends were provisionally twisted and perpendicularly soldered to the middle of the back, partially covering the juncture of the sheet metal edges. The front is decorated with several perpendicularly and horizontally arranged adjacent very thin double wires, some of which are smooth, while the others are sliced or coiled. The somewhat empty central square field bordered by these wide bands of wire displays an irregularly arranged, always differently placed thin ring of granules. The wires of the framing bands are each divided by two parallel rows of joined granules, while the diagonally placed rows of the same granules are soldered onto wires located above the lower decorative layer. At the ends and at the crossing point of the diagonal rows, wire rosettes with a large central granule were soldered, while on each side of the central rosette is a horizontal row of three widely spaced, irregular granules, which are missing on no. 7. In the middle of the rectangular, subsequently soldered bottom, the edges of the joints were covered with hammered silver wire, and a double smooth wire was placed lengthwise, and across it, alongside it, and along the edges rows of widely spaced granules were placed. The entire surface, outside and in, was gilded, including the entire decoration of soldered wires, while only the rosettes and the granulated part of the decoration were worked in silver. The gilt appears compact on the front side and in the interior of the container, while on the side and rear outside walls it is visible on a minimal surface. The handles are a little bent on all three examples, on the first the sheet metal on the right side is crumpled, the second has damage in the form of a regular circular hole on the bottom of the left side, and the third is crumpled in the lower right corner.

    Height: 38 and 41 mm
    Width: 27, 28, and 26 mm
    Thickness: 12 and 11 mm
    Weight: 6, 18, 6.08, and 5.58 gr
    (Fig. 3 a, b; Pl. I, 5, 6, 7)

8 – 9. A pair of pendants in the form of an axe with a single face. Thick smooth wire circlets were drawn through a narrow loop, with overlapping ends fixed with spiral coils. The spirals were formed from the thinned ends of the circlets after being pulled through the loop and were placed just next to it with a minimal gap to limit the movement of the pendant. The front side of the loop is formed into a parallelogram shaped smooth surface, bordered by horizontal folds, while the upper extension has a trapezoidal form and a straight serrated edge on the top. The lateral sides of the wide platelet of the pendant have a saddle-like curve, the edges are rounded, and the elongated blade is almost straight on the first example while it is rounded on the second. The front side of the platelet is bordered by grooves with a central band, and the same grooves are also carved within the border, where they are slanted on both sides, enclosing irregular triangular fields. The bands appear almost beaded and consist of rows of tiny parallelograms that rise from the deepened grooves and are at the level of the surface. Below the lower edging band, the blade is further decorated with double

slanted incisions in opposite directions forming adjacent triangles or a zigzag pattern. A row of five triple concentric circles was stamped above the band. Another such circle was placed at the top of the intersection of the two interior slanted grooves, with another two on top of the exterior grooves. The hoops on which the pendants hang have a rhomboid cross-section with rounded edges leading to a circular section on the thinned edges of the wire, wound around the circlets with five coils on the outer side of the spiral elements. On the first example, the oval tubular opening of the loop was made by piercing through the thickest part of the pendant with some instrument, while the opening was made on the second example by unforging the rear part of the loop, and riveting it to the back of the pendant with the aid of two rivets with hammered heads that are located above and below the opening of the loop.

Height: 44 and 43 mm
Width: 48 and 51 mm
Th. of the loop: 4 mm
Th. of the platelet: 1 mm
Dia.: hoop 25 and 29 mm
Weight: 10, 20, and 9.80 gr.
(Fig. 4 a, b; Pl. II, 8, 9)

10 – 18. Ten identical cylindrical beads of massive appearance, made from two types of differently formed circlets. The two outside and central circlets were made of silver wire, densely wound spirally, soldered and then hammered, with a hollow interior: they are somewhat flattened, but have a convex form on both sides, and their cross-section is close to an ellipse. Between the wire circlets – the middle and two outer – two narrower circlets were soldered, made from a band of silver sheet metal curved in a ring shape. The bands were joined by soldering in various spots, with a space and not at the same spot of the upright axis. At both ends, i.e. at the site of the join with the wire rings, the sheet metal bands were bordered with a smooth double hammered silver wire, and within this edge, large silver granules were soldered with irregular spacing. The edges of the exterior borders of the wire rings were set with silver wire onto which rows of tiny silver joined granules were soldered. Of the external sections, it appears that only the surface of the sheet-metal circlets was gilded, below the edges and the granules, while the interior of the beads was completely gilded. The interior gilt has a dull yellow matte colour, while the shininess of the exterior gilt is more intensive. Example no. 8 is damaged on one outer edge, and a few small granules have been lost; on example no. 9, one end is a little flattened, and part of the edge granulation is missing on the other; no. 10 is deformed, part is missing from one end, and on the other end almost half of the exterior wire ring is missing; no. 11 is slightly crooked on one end, as is also true for no. 14 and no. 15; on no. 13, a few of the edging granules are missing, and the sheet metal is perforated on one of the banded rings.

Length: 15 - 17 mm
Dia.: 15 and 16 mm
Thickness: 2 mm
Weight: 3.48 - 4.22 gr (total weight: 35.19 gr)
(Fig. 5; Pl. II, 10 - 18)

19. A flexible chain necklace with an internal hollow constructed from six joined smooth bands of wires braided into a plait with a filigree decoration on the ends and on the clasp. The ends of the chain are enclosed by cylindrical tubular clamp elements formed from sheet metal parallelograms, with precisely cut ends and seams carefully joined by soldering. On both ends and in the middle of the tubular terminals are shallow ring-shaped bands, made of triple soldered and hammered wire, while the area between them is divided by slanted soldered and hammered pieces of smooth wire, which form elongated oppositely arranged empty triangular fields. The outer end of each tube is closed off by sheet-metal from which a banded ribbed circular loop extends. Through each loop is threaded a large ring-like circlet with joined ends, onto which a double loop is attached on one side of the chain, and a loop with a hook on the other. Like the circlets, the loops and hook are massive, made from metal rods of circular section. Circular platelets with a flat edge were soldered onto the middle of the loop and hook and also the double loop. The circlets are decorated with a ring of

joined granules, and above this was a domed section, decorated with five curved pieces of wire in the form of shallow arcades, forming a circular frame on the top with a large granule on the peak in the centre. The wire is not uniform, in places it is smooth or slightly twisted or denticulated. The gilt is partially preserved on the surface of the circular platelets. The exterior visible side of the hook is decorated by a central groove with a band of bead-like appearance, worked identically to those on pendants nos. 8 and 9. The end section of the hook is thinned and broadened like a beak, and its barely emphasized zoomorphic appearance is supplemented from the side views, with double concentric circles in place of eyes, the exterior one – too large for the thickness of the profile – incompletely stamped. One of the five small arcades on the domed button above the hook is poorly formed and was soldered upside down. The woven chain had been broken at the juncture with one tubular clamp – on the end with the double loop – and it was reattached in a recent restoration attempt, when one domed button was also reattached.

Length of the chain: ca. 335 mm
Dia. of the chain: 8 mm
Length of the tubular clamp ends: 34 and 33 mm
Length of the hook and eye: 57 and 58 mm
Dia. of the domed buttons: 16 mm
Weight: 96.20 gr
(Fig. 6 a, b; Pl. III, 19)

20. A neck ring made from a smoothly cast rod of irregular rhomboid-oval section, with engraved decoration not merely on the ends but also on the exterior part of the widest section of the torc. The torc narrows towards the ends, which are hammered flat and shaped into snake heads. The neck, separated from the head by slanted double grooves with joined tops, is decorated further with triple slanted grooves in two directions, alternating with stamped circles with a central point, corresponding to the design of the eyes, and along the outside of the lateral lengthwise grooves on the head three and four, respectively, points were stamped. On the part of the torc opposite the ends, the decoration consists of two exterior segments, 2 cm long, covered with a row of slanted crossed lines like the letter "x", a central segment around 3 cm long, with two rows of slanted lines in opposite directions separated by an incised lengthwise line, representing a herringbone or pine branch motif, while between the segments are stamped circles with a central point. The torc is slightly deformed.

Dia.: 125 mm
Th.: 6 mm
Width of ends: 3 mm
Dim. snake heads: 15 x 8 mm
Weight: 42.90 gr
(Fig. 7 a, b; Pl. IV, 20)

21. A neck ring made from a bar of square section with sharp edges and a deep smooth groove incised on all four sides. One half of such divided elongated surfaces – on two opposite sites – was incised with slanted lines, and then the bar was spirally twisted. In this manner each second twisted section of the torc is covered with slanted incisions. The untwisted thinned ends, of rectangular section, were decorated on the exterior visible side – in an area of ca. 4 cm – with a dense irregular row of connected lines (tremolo motif), which extends to the beginning of the spiral twisting. The ends were hammered flat and shaped into snake heads, similar to those on the previous example, no. 20. The circles with the point in place of the eyes were more poorly made, and the horizontal rows of points were stamped over the lengthwise grooves. The final edge of the snake head on the right end is not rounded, but straight, and the tremulous line is interrupted in the first third and is more irregular.

Dia.: 154 mm
Thickness: 8 mm
Width of ends: 4 mm
Dim. snake heads: 14 x 8 mm

Weight: 80.00 gr
(Fig. 8 a, b; Pl. V, 21)

22. A neck ring made from a bar of square section with sharp edges, worked in the same manner as the previous no. 21. The incised lines on the halves of the opposing sides of the bar, divided by grooves, are irregularly spaced and in some places look like commas. The exterior surfaces of the flatly hammered ends – in a length of ca. 5.5 cm – are covered to the edges with a dense irregular net of slanted crossed lines (hatching). The snake heads are similar to the previous examples. The point within the circle at the place of the eyes was shallowly stamped, horizontal lines of points were stamped over the lengthwise grooves on the head and over slanted grooves on the neck, forming the letter V. The lines of the spiral twisting are distorted in places, as is the torc itself.

Dia.: 168 mm
Thickness: 8 mm
Width of ends: 5 mm
Dim. snake heads: 16 x 9 mm
Weight: 99.80 gr
(Fig. 9 a, b; Pl. VI, 22)

23. A neck ring made from a bar of square section, with incised grooves on all four sides. The dense spiral twisting on the thickest part of the ring is rounded on the inner side, while on the outside the edges retained a reduced sharpness. The elongated, thin hammered ends in the form of a stretched ellipse terminate in a drop-like section with an impressed triangular hollow. At a small distance from the spiral twisting – in a section ca. 6 cm long – the ends are decorated by a lengthwise central, somewhat uneven row of hollows similar in form to a reversed letter S. Unattached double slanted grooves are carved on both sides of the central row, marking off triangular and rhomboid fields.

Dia.: 137 mm
Thickness: 6 mm
Dim. of the ends: 65 x 6 mm
Weight: 33.82 gr
(Fig. 10 a, b; Pl. VII, 23)

24. A neck ring from a four-edged rod, manufactured like the previous example, no. 23, including the engraved decoration on the similarly formed ends. The spiral twisting is not uniform, as the spirals are tighter towards the ends, while the edges remain quite sharp throughout the entire length. The decoration of the ends, located in an area ca. 6.5 cm long, was poorly carried out, as neither the distances nor directions are strictly respected, for the central row of reverse S-like symbols, or for the single and multiple slanted incisions. The teardrop terminal of the right end is formed with an elevated surface with a cross incision. The line of the torc is distorted, as is part of the spiral twisting on the left side of the torc.

Dia.: 157 mm
Thickness: 7 mm
Dim. of the ends: 70 x 11 mm
Weight: 79.20 gr
(Fig. 11 a, b; Pl. VIII, 24)

25. A neck ring, like the two previous examples, nos. 23 and 24. The uniformly spiral twists are mostly rounded, while only in places did the angled edges retain a slightly reduced sharpness. The decoration on the ends with smooth drop-like terminals, located in a band of ca. 6 cm in length, was carefully worked in relation to the stamped lengthwise row, but was burnished on the surface or highly worn.

Dia.: 143 mm

Thickness: 6 mm
Dim. of the ends: 63 x 7 mm
Weight: 32.50 gr
(Fig. 12 a, b; Pl. IX, 25)

26. A neck ring with sharp edges, like the three previous examples, nos. 23. – 25. The spiral twisting is not uniform and lacks rhythm, while the line of the torc is slightly deformed, and the ends have no decoration. It appears to be an unfinished or unsuccessful example.

Dia.: 147 mm
Thickness: 7 mm
Dim. of the ends: 68 x 10 mm
Weight: 72.30 gr
(Fig. 13 a, b; Pl. X, 26)

27. A neck ring, made in the manner of the previous examples: a bar of square section, divided on all four sides with a central lengthwise groove, and then spirally twisted. The spirals are closely packed, with a regular rhythm, the edges are finely rounded, and only in places can a blunted edge be seen, while in the narrowed sections the edges are entirely flattened and straight. The banded ends are hammered flat and have well-fashioned rounded drop-shaped endings. From the last spiral to the smooth end, in a length of ca. 6 cm, a decoration was carried out with particular attention, composed of a dense row of points along each edge, with a wavy line of points between them and seven concentric circles located in the six non-identical curves. One end is slightly cracked, and the other had been broken off and was recently soldered back into place.

Dia.: 136 mm
Thickness: 7 mm
Dim. of the ends: 64 x 5 mm
Weight: 52.10 gr
(Fig. 14 a, b; Pl. XI, 27)

28. A neck ring, made similarly as the previous examples. The spiral twists are stretched in the thickest part of the ring, and denser towards the ends, and in general are rounded and have the appearance of separate thin bars of circular section. The long narrow flattened bands of the ends have smooth thin curled round terminals. The decoration, engraved in a length of ca. 4 cm, which covers half of the ends, consists of a lengthwise groove with slanted lines in opposite directions on both sides, in a herringbone pattern. One end is slightly deformed.

Dia.: 131 mm
Thickness: 6 mm
Dim. of the ends: 70 x 4 mm
Weight: 35.70 gr
(Fig. 15 a, b; Pl. XII, 28)

29. An incomplete neck ring, with regular rounded spiral twisting, made in the same manner as the previous examples. The banded ends are decorated with a central interrupted lengthwise row of impressed points, in places missing or worn. One end of the torc is broken, the other has a damaged edge, and both terminals are broken off the ends.

Dia.: 119 mm
Thickness: 7 mm
Width of the ends: 3 mm
Weight: 30.70 gr
(Fig. 16 a, b; Pl. XIII, 29)

30. A neck ring, made from a bar of square section all four sides of which were divided by a lengthwise groove prior to spiral twisting. The twists are denser towards the ends, and all have sharp angled edges. The ends are hammered flat and smooth, widened towards the terminals and cut off straight in the widest part, each with one circular perforation. The perpendicular edge is damaged on one of the ends.

   Dia.: 153 mm
   Thickness: 10 mm
   Dim. of the ends: 68 x 14 mm
   Weight: 95.50 gr
   (Fig. 17 a, b; Pl. XIV, 30)

31. A neck ring with trapezoidal widened ends, each with a circular perforation. It was made in the same manner as the previous no. 30, and also has sharp edges on the spirals. On the edges of the lengthwise grooves carved into the surfaces of the rod, traces of the instrument used to remove the metal were not removed and are visible everywhere: the traces look like commas, and in places like a denticulated row. The widened flat ends are entirely covered by engraved decoration in a length of ca. 7.5 cm. They are framed by an irregular row along the edges composed of small, connected triangular hollows. The area within the borders is divided into several fields separated by perpendicular lines. In two fields in the broad part of the ends, triple concentric circles were stamped one above another, with a circular perforation between. The narrower part, separated by beginning and ending fields decorated with horizontal lightly incised lines, is filled with two rows of irregularly arranged concentric circles, the upper one interrupted. Beyond the border on the broadest part are carelessly engraved slanted lines in both directions, while the very edge of the terminals is covered with short horizontal incisions.

   Dia.: 194 mm
   Thickness: 12 mm
   Dim. of the ends: 78 and 81 x 17 mm
   Weight: 137.40 gr
   (Fig. 18 a, b; Pl. XV, 31)

32. A banded bracelet with widened and snake head shaped ends. The hoop is flat inside, and slightly rounded on the outside; the rounded hoop merges into a barely visible central rib on the ends, which are not entirely flat. The ends are decorated in a length of ca. 3 cm with double slanted and crossed lines that mark off rhomboid fields. The snake heads are bordered by rows of tiny stamped points, with irregular semicircular and square miniature areas between, giving the effect of a beaded motif. The eyes on the stylized head were marked by closely spaced triple concentric circles. The borders cease at the corners, where the edges of the ends are damaged.

   Dia.: 65 mm
   Thickness of the hoop and ends: 1 mm
   Dim. of the ends: 23 x 12 mm
   Weight: 8.50 gr
   (Fig. 19; Pl. XVI, 32)

33. A bracelet similar to the preceding one, made of sheet metal still sufficiently elastic to permit movement of the ends. It represents the only example with a somewhat different, yellowish nuance with a dark shine. The banded hoop is slightly bent inside and rounded on the outside, while towards the ends it merges into the straight and flat ends. The stylized snake heads have a rhomboid form, bordered by rows along the edges based on motifs as for the previous example no. 32, imitating a beaded band. An identical horizontal lengthwise row divides the rhomb into two triangles, with double circles shallowly stamped, with the inner one almost invisible. Further, the edge rows continue into smooth grooves in the same direction, which in a length of ca. 5 mm decorate the final sections of the hoop, filled with tiny impressed circles. The hoop is slightly deformed, the surface is uneven, in places corroded, and the edges of the ends are insignificantly damaged.

Dia.: 61 mm
Thickness of the hoop and ends: 0.5 mm
Dim. of the ends: 30 x 16 mm
Weight: 7.70 gr
(Fig. 20; Pl. XVI, 33)

34 – 35. A pair of sheet metal bracelets with zoomorphic ends. The broad banded hoop, like the central lengthwise part of the ends, were hammered over a rounded backing and are gently rounded on the exterior side. The ends are quite widened in the beginning section, where there is an ear-like rounding, and the surface is divided with lengthwise double grooves and triple perpendicular ones. All the grooves were engraved not at once, but in several short passes.

Dia.: 60 and 62 mm
Thickness of the hoop and ends: 1 and 0.5 mm
Dim. of the ends: 27 x 16 and 17 mm
Weight: 10.60 and 10.70 gr
(Fig. 21; Pl. XVI, 34 - 35)

36 – 37. A pair of somewhat larger sheet metal bracelets, identical to the previous examples, nos. 34 and 35, both in terms of the workmanship and the state of preservation.

Dia.: 65 and 63 mm
Thickness of the hoop and ends: 1 and 0.5 mm
Dim. of the ends: 30 x 20 mm
Weight: 15.90 and 16.20 gr
(Fig. 22; Pl. XVI, 36 - 37)

38 – 39. A pair of bracelets made from massive rod of irregular circular section, with slightly emphasized edges on both sides. The hoop is somewhat thicker in the middle, and is thinned towards the ends with rounded terminals. Traces of forging are visible on the surface of the hoop.

Dia.: 68 mm
Thickness: 4 and 5 mm
Weight: 21.50 and 20.20 gr
(Fig. 23 a, b; Pl. XVII, 38 - 39)

40 – 41. A pair of smaller bracelets identical to the previous nos. 38 and 39. They were made from thick wire withy a variable circular section. The thickness of the hoop is uniform and oscillated minimally, while the ends were cut straight.

Dia.: 64 and 58 mm
Thickness: 2 – 3 mm
Weight: 8.50 and 7.50 gr
(Fig. 24; Pl. XVII, 40 - 41)

42. A tripartite sheet metal pendant with embossed decoration. It is composed of a large crescent shaped plate, which is bordered – along the outer and inner edges – with a double row of short oblique ribbed protrusions facing in opposite directions, with a dense row of bead-like protrusions between them. Above the lower or interior edge are two more segments of the same border. Between them is a smooth dome ringed by a bead-like row, and two similar dome elements are also located on the arms of the large crescent pendant. Above each dome is one thin, slightly embossed crescent, with a larger beaded row on its surface. Between the thin crescents are two thicker crescents with protruding edges and a depressed central section, where a bead-like row was impressed. Both of the interior pendants – the larger crescent-shaped one, and the small leaf-shaped

one – are decorated with smooth domed elements ringed by beads, three on the former and one on the latter. The ends of the arms on all three pendant elements – as well as on all remaining pendants of the set – are rounded and variously formed: drop-shaped, hemispherical, or flattened, sometimes with signs of pseudo-moulding. The interior pendants are suspended with the help of long banded bent hooks on the back, which were pulled through irregular circular openings. The large upper crescent pendant, with a badly centred perforation at the top of the platelet, is hung – with a short wire "noose" – from a closed square wire element with overlapping ends. On each side of this square wire are attached two sheet metal tubes of circular section, made from cut parallelograms of very thin sheet metal, whose lengthwise ends are merely joined together on the rear. All the tubes, which have two perforations on each side, were curled around equally long wooden rods, pieces of which are still preserved in the interior of both lower tubes. The decoration, embossed onto the sheet metal before it was rolled into a tube, has a somewhat reduced plasticity, and consists of rows of rib-like protrusions and oblique moulding, located between the perpendicular edge and interior moulding. All the moulding was formed from double smooth folds with a beaded row in the intermediate area. The sheet metal is slightly cracked on the left arm of the large upper crescent pendant, a large part of the bent hook on the back of the central pendant is broken off, the edges of the openings on the tubes are damaged, and some of the perforations on them are torn.

Dim. upper pendant: 71 x 73 x 0.5 mm
Dim. central pendant: 35 x 35 x 1 mm
Dim. lower pendant: 14 x 25 x 0.5 mm
Length tubes: 55 – 58 mm
Dia. tubes: 10 – 11 mm
Weight: 30.60 gr
(Fig. 25 a, b; Pl. XVIII, 42)

43. A somewhat smaller tripartite pendant resembling no. 42. The exterior crescent-shaped pendant element is decorated with two narrow beaded lunulae, located to each side of the central domed element, while above it and directly adjacent to it is a smooth relief lunula, which appears only on this example. Part of the inner row of ribbed protrusions of the border is omitted on the left arm of the large pendant. A wire noose with a double loop is threaded through a poorly centred upper perforation on the large pendant. The pair of sheet metal cylinders are somewhat longer than those on the previous example no. 42, and they also have longer folded-over crooked edges on the rear, joined by a piece of hammered wire threaded through a spot closer to the right half: the upper part of the wire is joined to the sheet metal of the upper tube, and the lower part is formed into a hook onto which a single-looped noose with a broken end is connected. Sections of square shaped wires were drawn through lateral perforations on both joined cylinders, and onto them elongated polyhedral beads were threaded with polished rhomboid and triangular planes, now worn facets. The beads are made of opaque dark blue glass paste, in a shade close to cobalt. The small wooden rods placed in the interior of the cylinders to prevent deformation of the sheet metal, without which the tubes could not retain their original form, are almost entirely preserved. Part of the single looped noose is missing, as well as parts of both square wire elements, while the edges of the openings on the cylinders are badly damaged and some are torn.

Dim. of the upper pendant: 66 x 63 x 0.5 mm
Dim. of the middle pendant: 31 x 33 x 1 mm
Dim. of the lower pendant: 14 x 25 x 0.5 mm
Length of the tubes: 81 and 82 mm
Dia. of the tubes: 10 and 11 mm
Dim. of the beads: 14 x 7 and 16 x 7 mm
Weight: 32.90 gr (with beads)
(Fig. 26 a, b; Pl. XIX, 43)

44. A tripartite pendant, identical to the previous example no. 43. The beaded lunula below the perforation for suspension on the large pendant is joined to the central domed element. The interior ribbed row on the border around the lower edge is missing, while the exterior row was not embossed around the V-shaped opening. The cylinders with the interior wooden rods almost entirely preserved

are perforated – nearer the left end – by a wire hook, another hook with two loops hanging from it, the lower one broken. A fragment of a blue bead is threaded onto the completely preserved square wire element on the left. Almost all the square wire element is missing on the right. The left arm of the largest pendant was broken off and was recently soldered back on, and on the rear of the lower cylinder, the sheet metal is pierced.

Dim. of the upper pendant: 64 x 64 x 0.5 mm
Dim. of the middle pendant: 30 x 32 x 0.5 mm
Dim. of the lower pendant: 13 x 26 x 0.5 mm
Length of the tubes: 77 mm
Dia. of the tubes: 10 and 11 mm
Weight: 32.00 gr (with the piece of bead)
(Fig. 27; Pl. XX, 44)

45. A two-part pendant, composed of a large crescent-shaped pendant identical to those on the previous examples, and a smaller pendant, circular and leaf-shaped. The lower row of ribbed protrusions is not embossed on the border along the upper edge of the large pendant, and they are also missing on the arms. The "noose" for hanging is completely deformed, the upper loop is uncoiled, and the lower one formed into a provisory hook.

Dim. of the upper pendant: 66 x 59 x 0.5 mm
Dim. of the lower pendant: 23 x 39 x 0.5 mm
Weight: 14.20 gr
(Fig. 28 a, b; Pl. XXI, 45)

46. A two-part pendant, similar to no. 44, including the too elevated central beaded lunula, which touches the edge of the opening for suspension. The border around the upper edge is complete, while around the lower edge, the sections of the upper ribbed row are missing on the end of the arms. The beaded row around the domed element on the lower pendant was in places poorly embossed, and in an attempt at correction was duplicated on the left side. The opening for suspending the large pendant is torn, and only the lower loop is preserved from the noose-like element for hanging.

Dim. of the upper pendant: 62 x 61 x 0.5 mm
Dim. of the lower pendant: 25 x 39 x 0.5 mm
Weight: 10.70 gr
(Fig. 29; Pl. XXI, 46)

Plate I

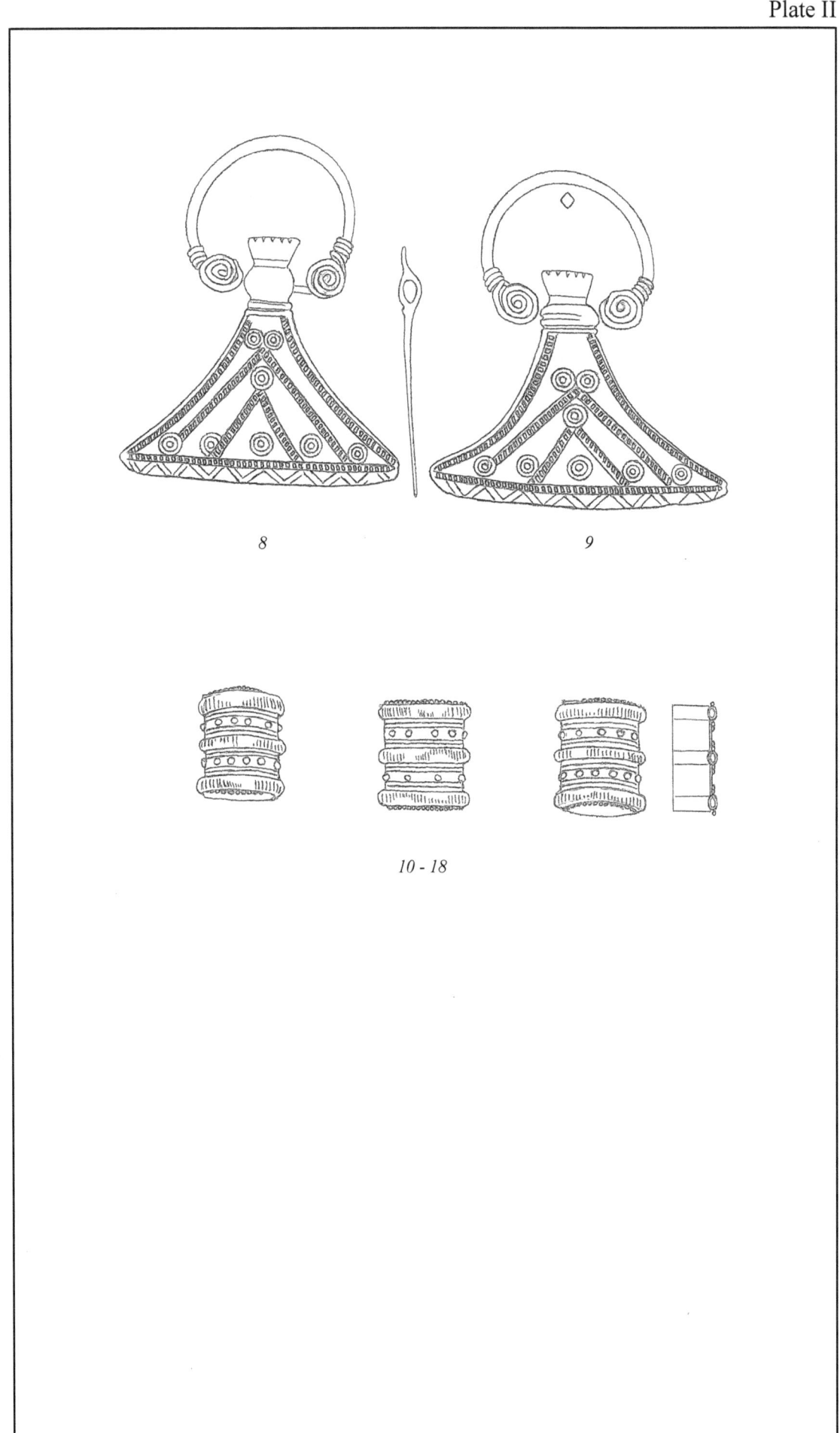

Plate II

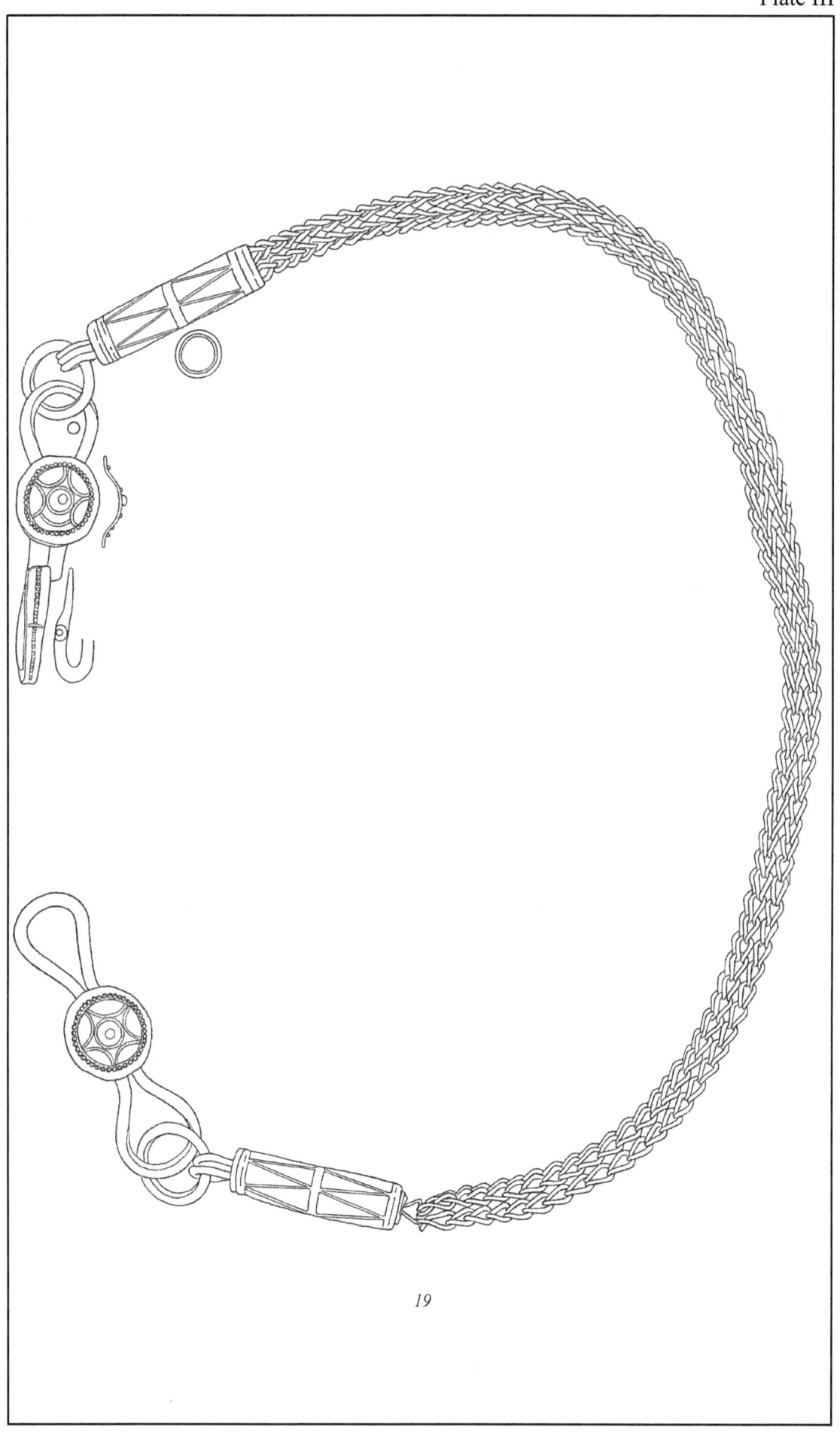

19

Plate IV

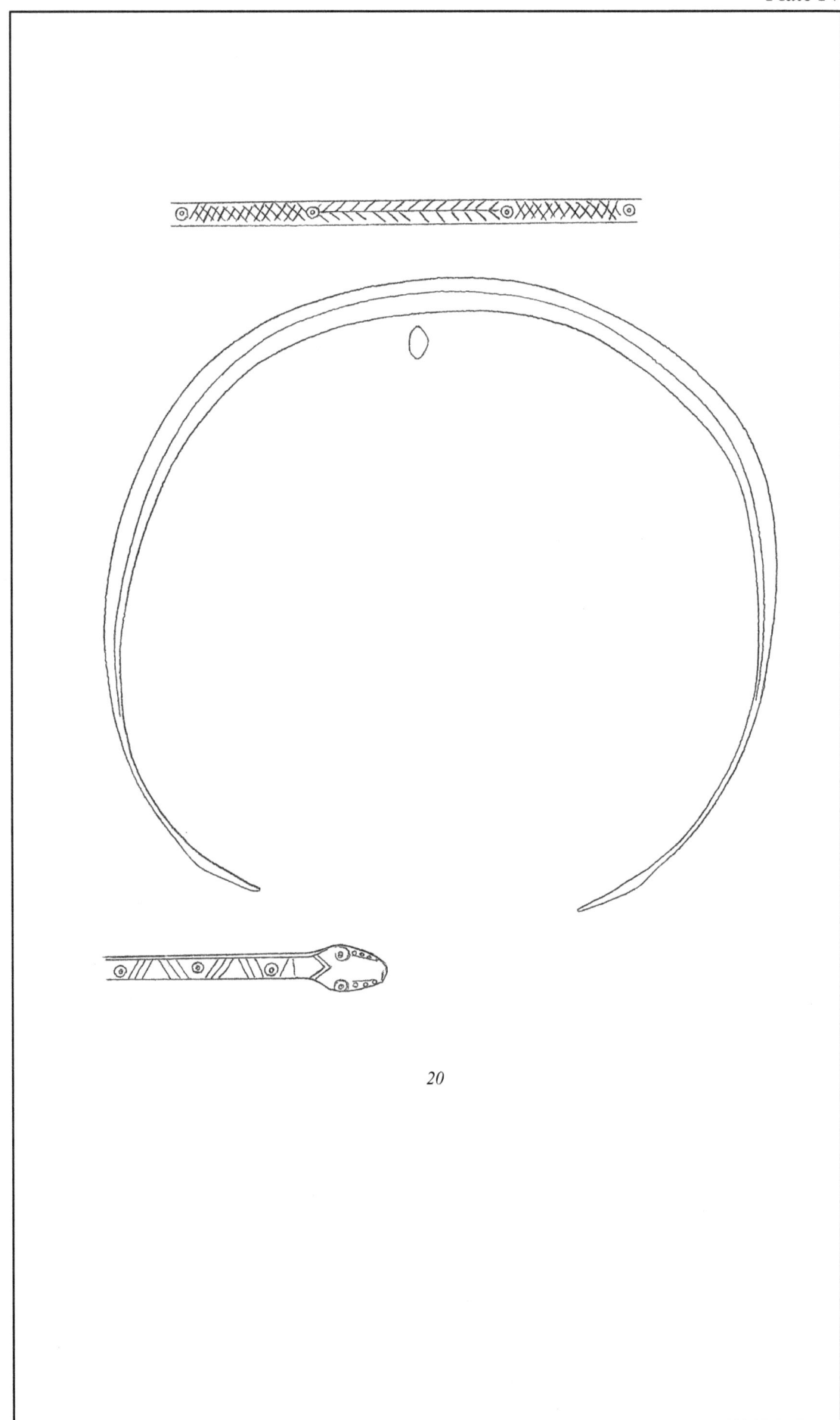

20

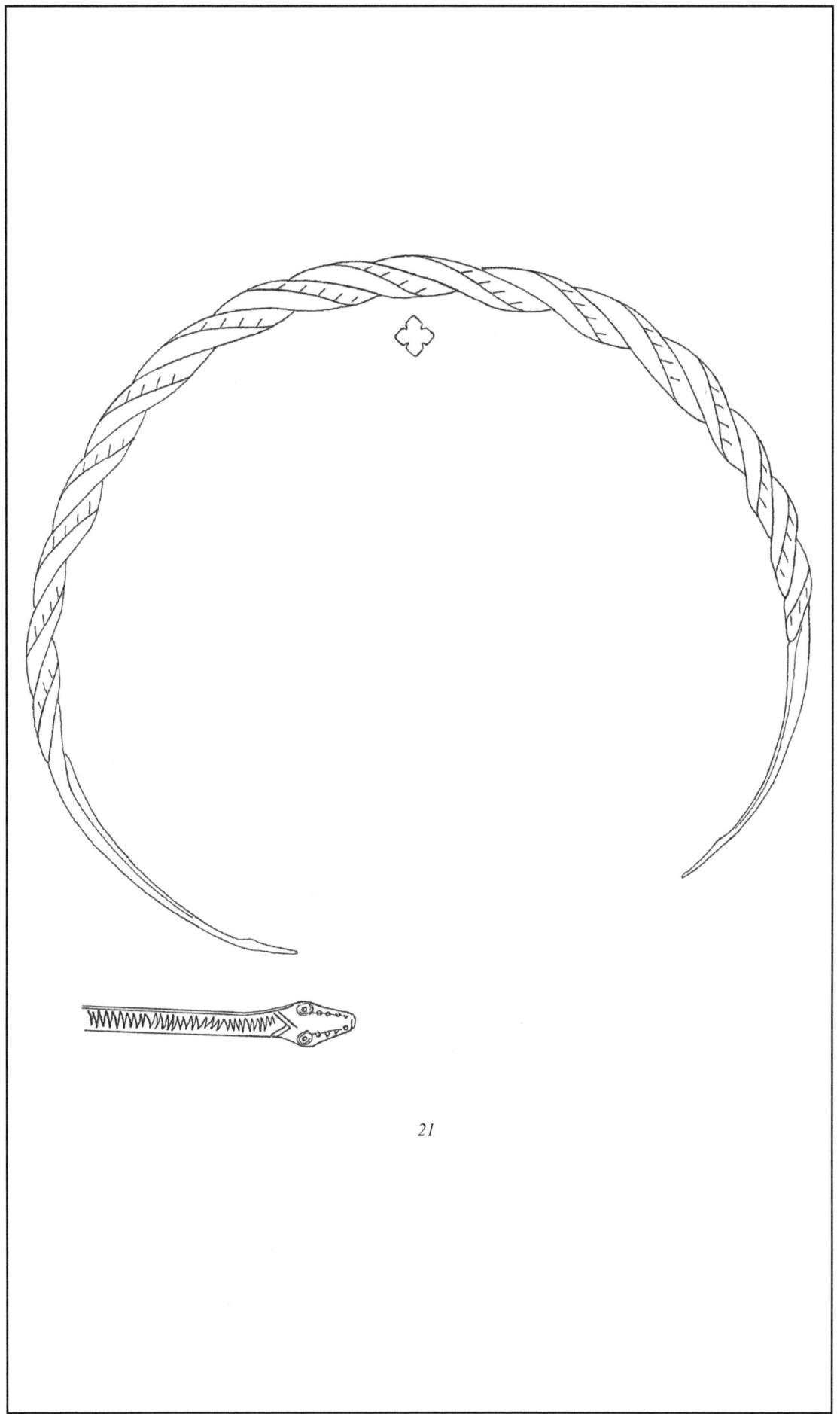

21

A Roman Hoard of Silver Jewellery

Plate VI

22

Plate VII

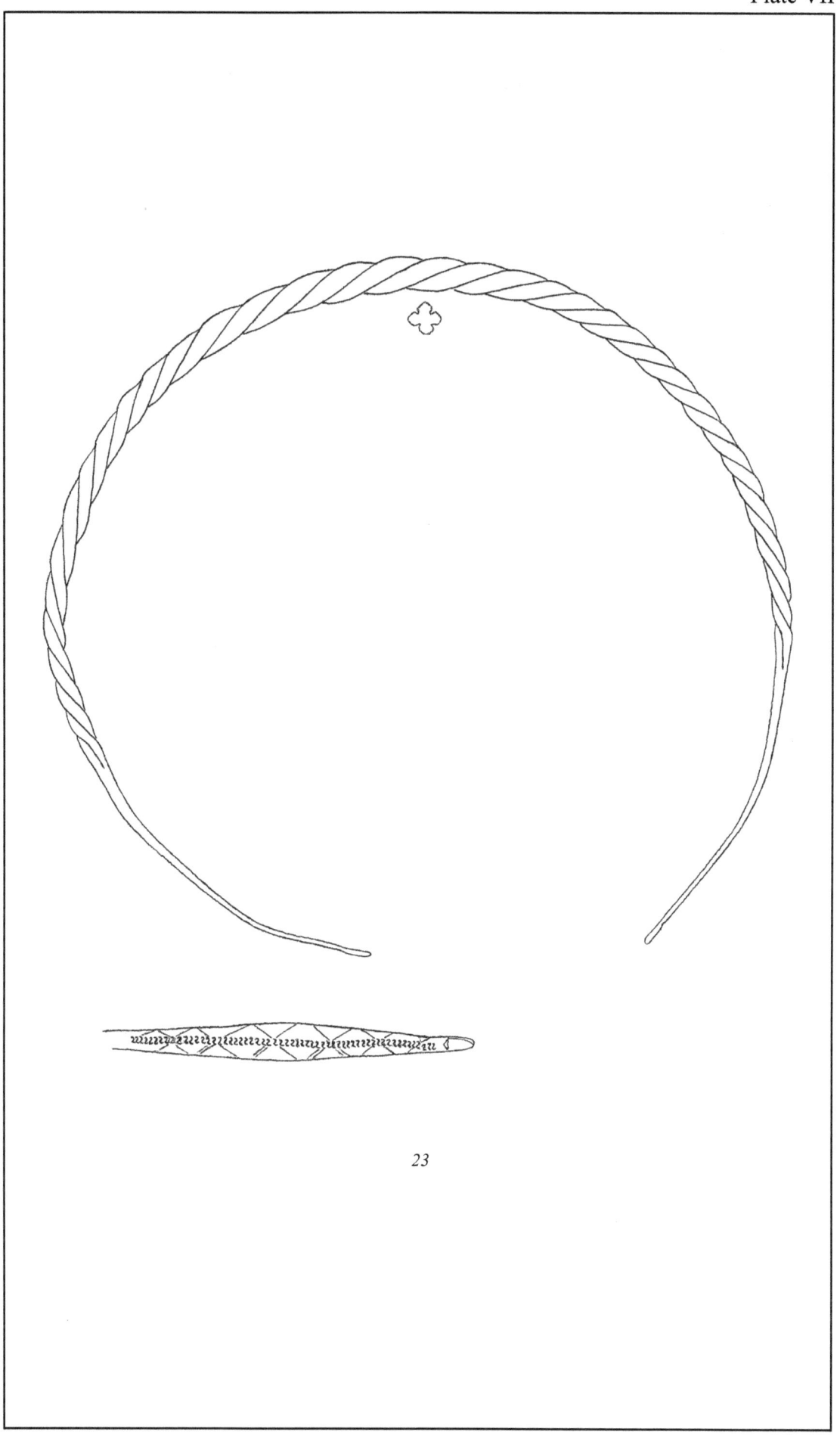

23

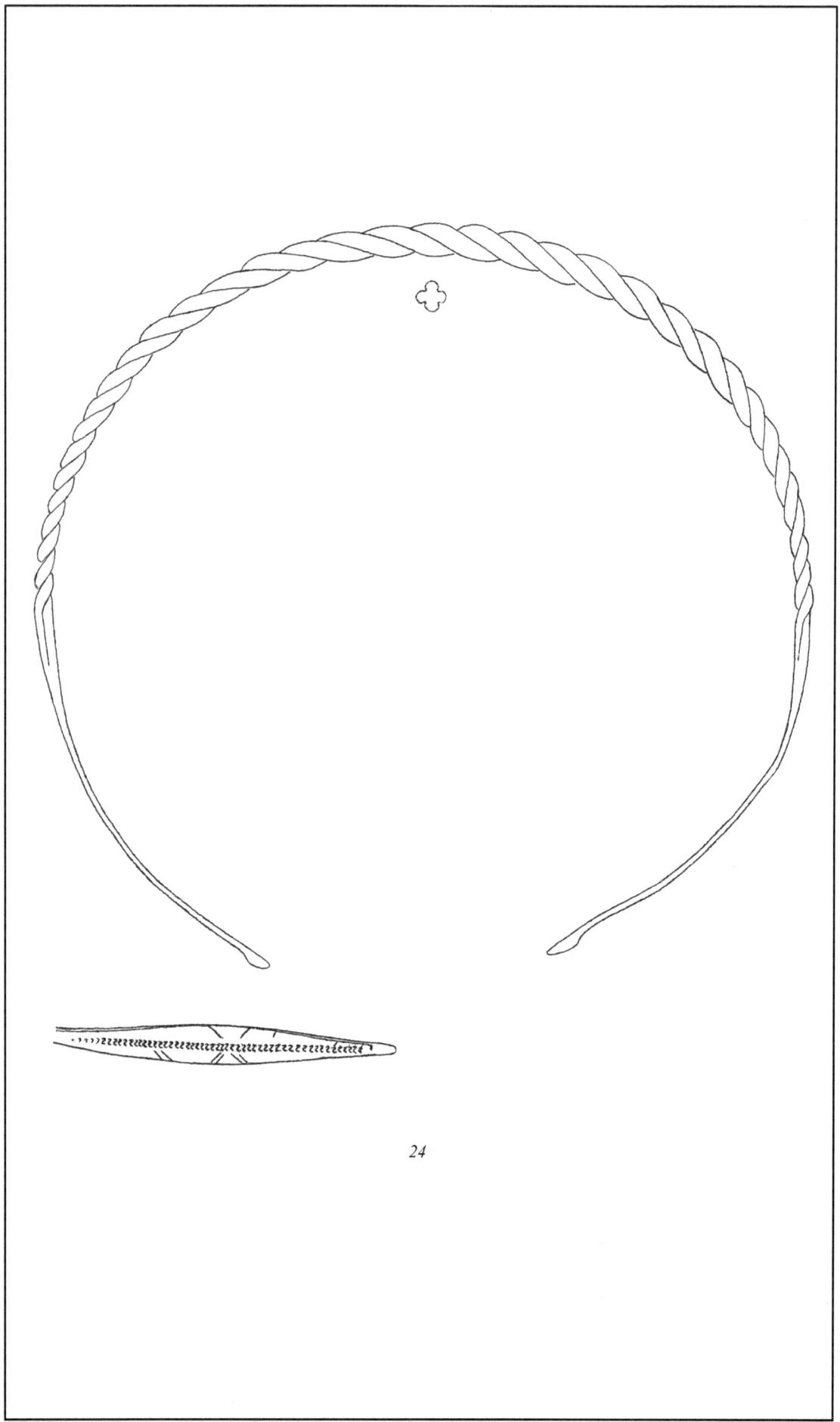

24

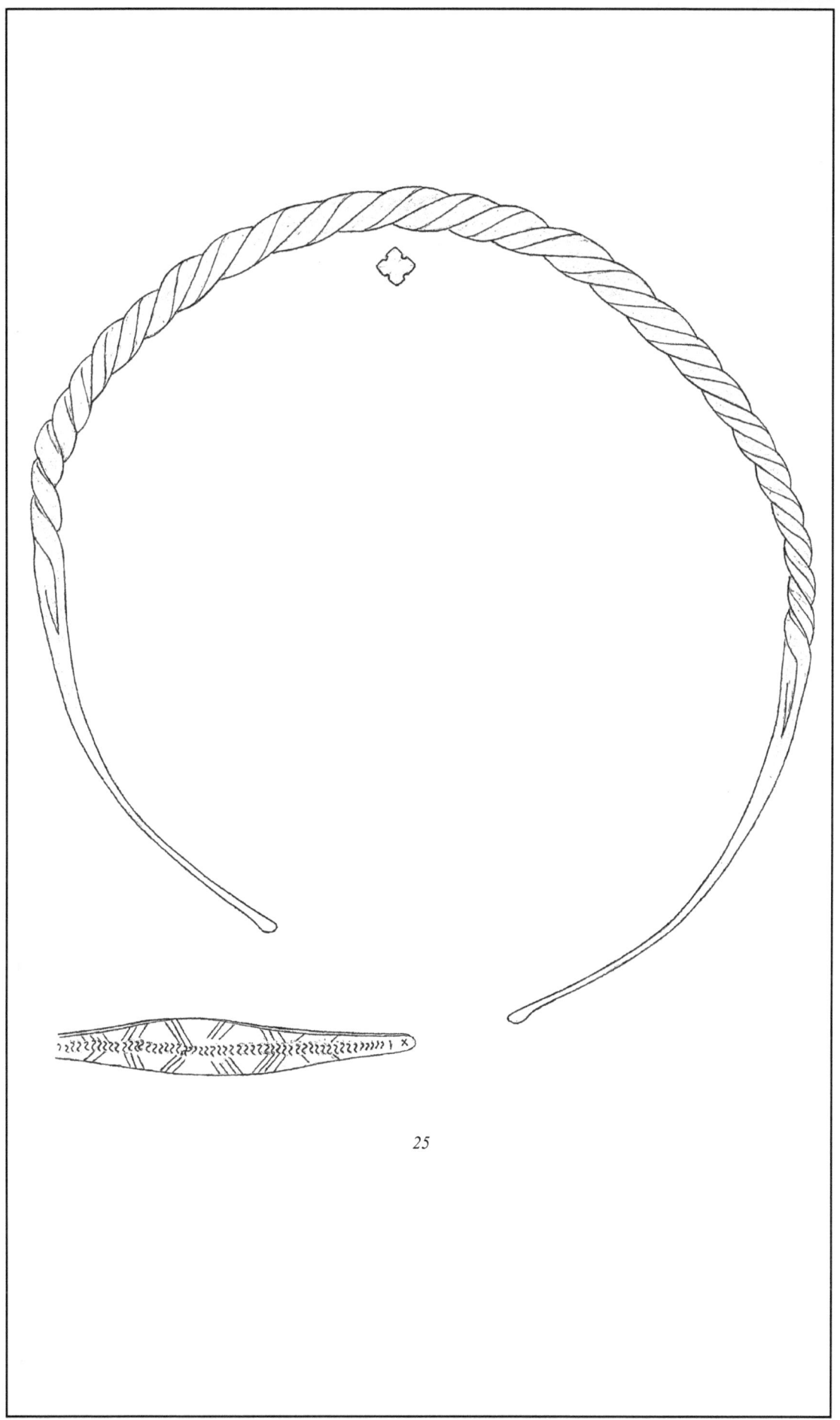

26

Remza Koščević

Plate XI

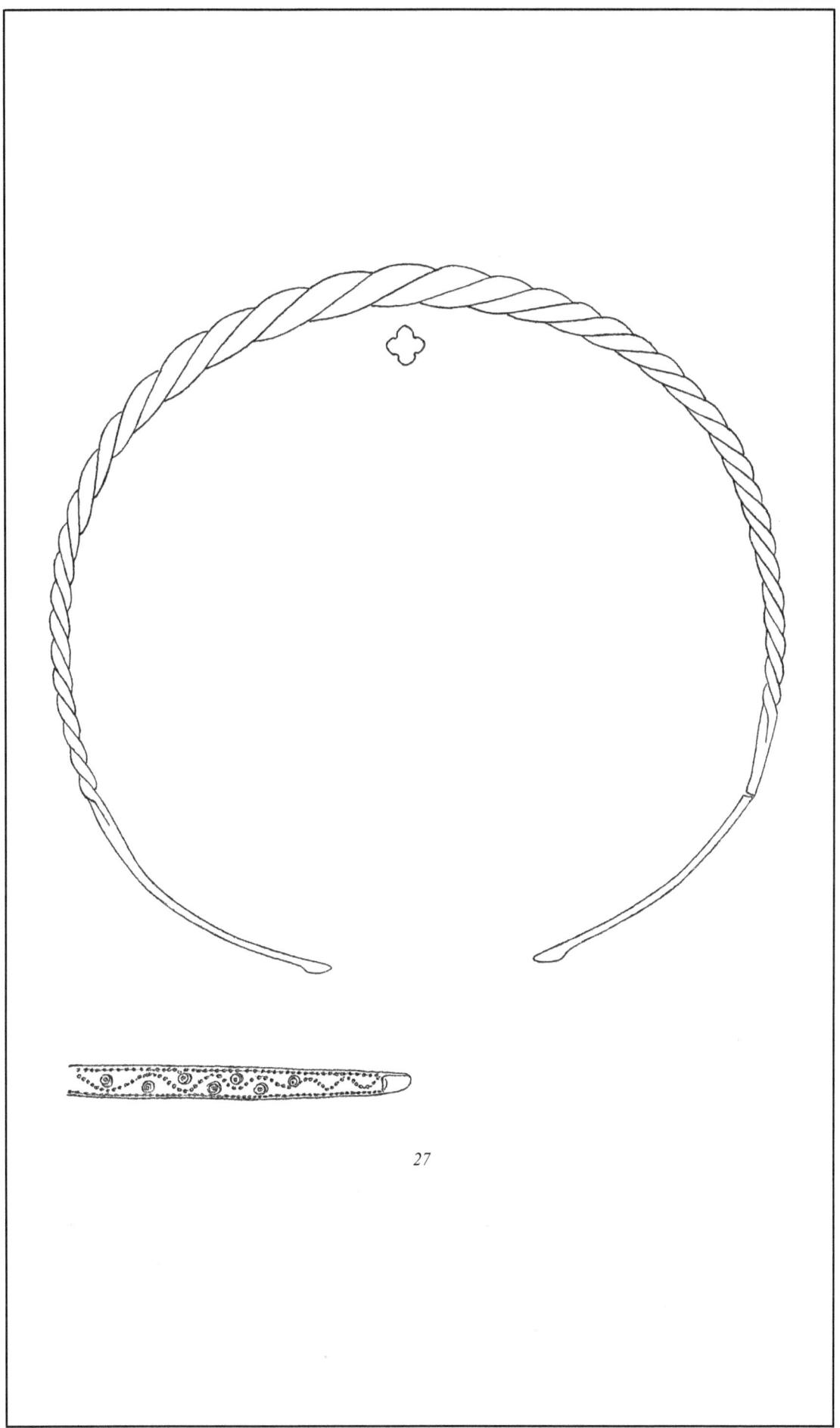

27

A Roman Hoard of Silver Jewellery

Plate XII

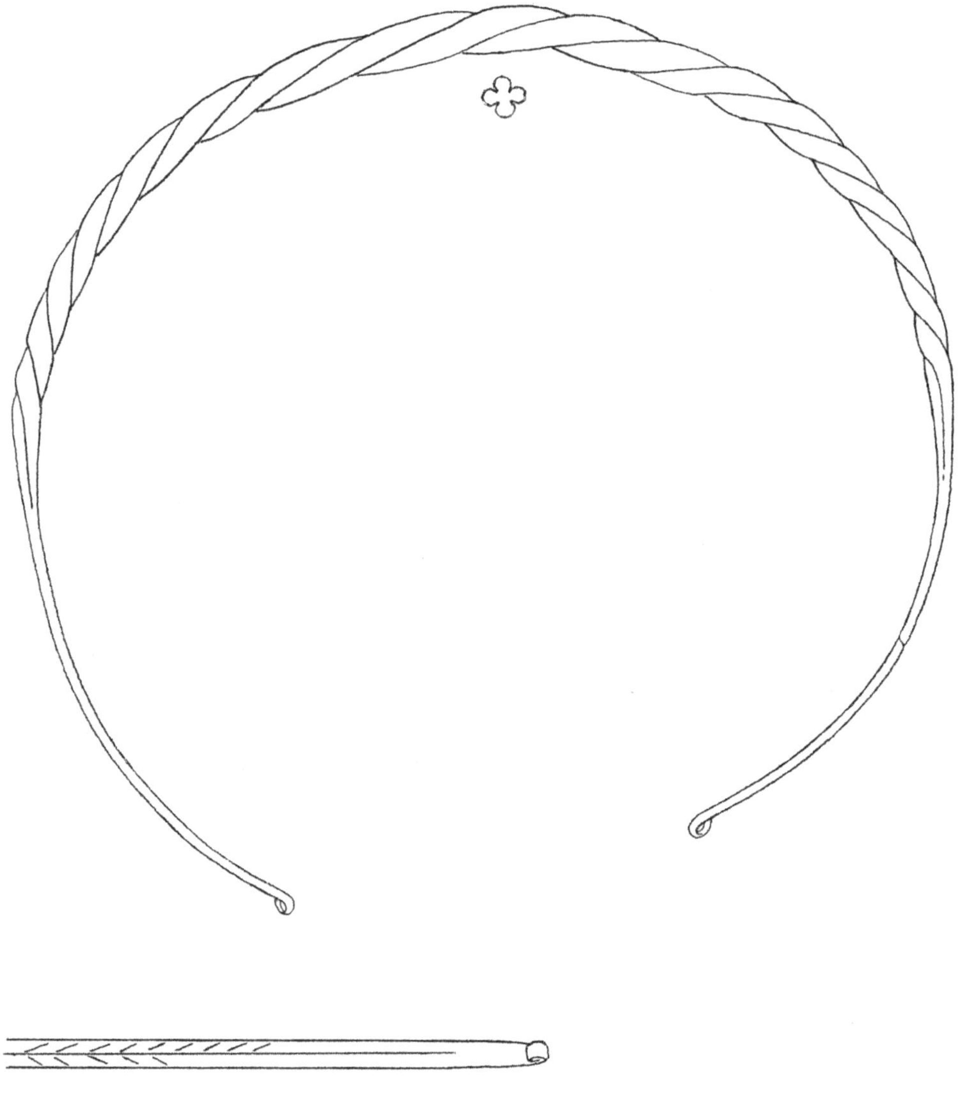

28

Plate XIII

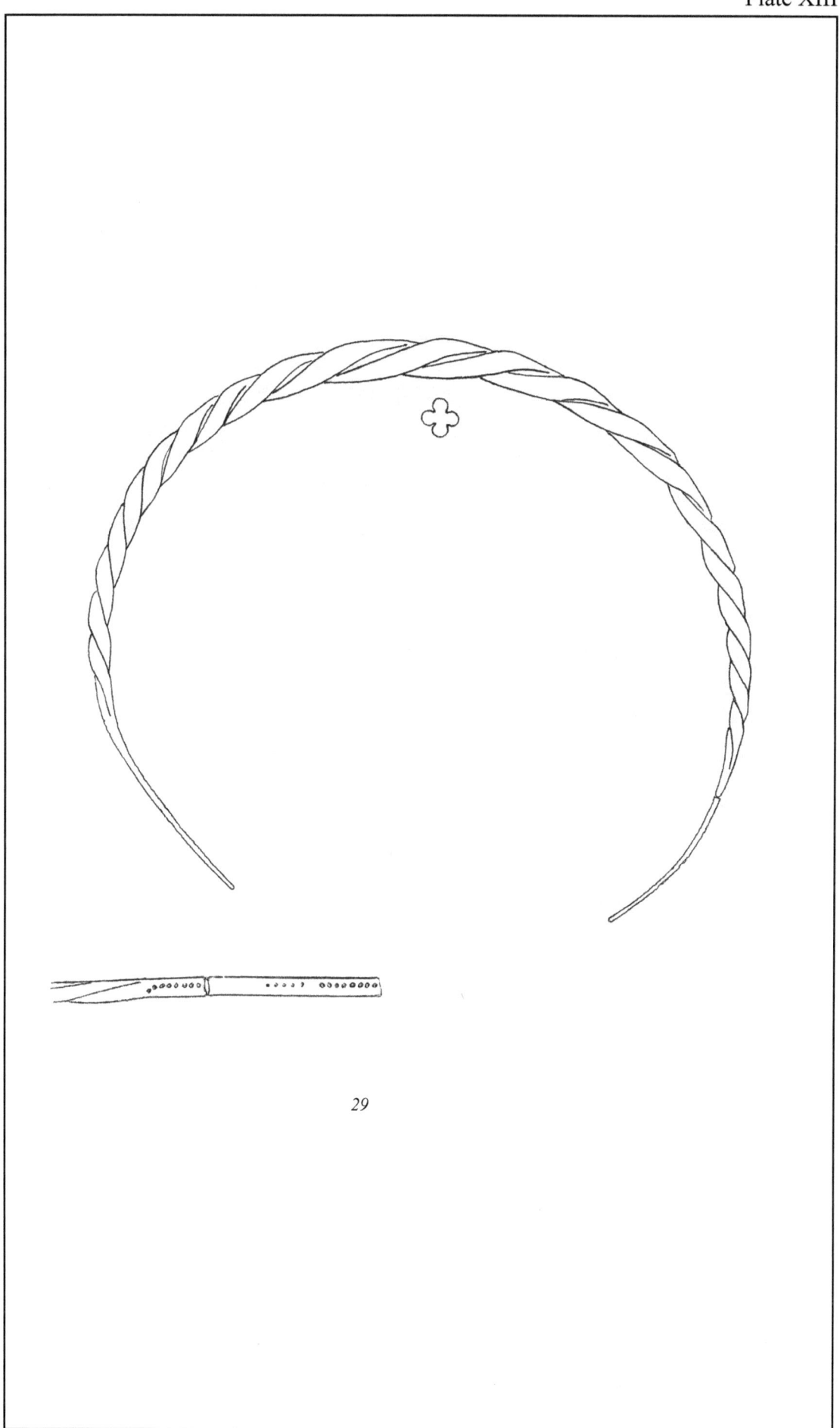

29

A Roman Hoard of Silver Jewellery

Plate XIV

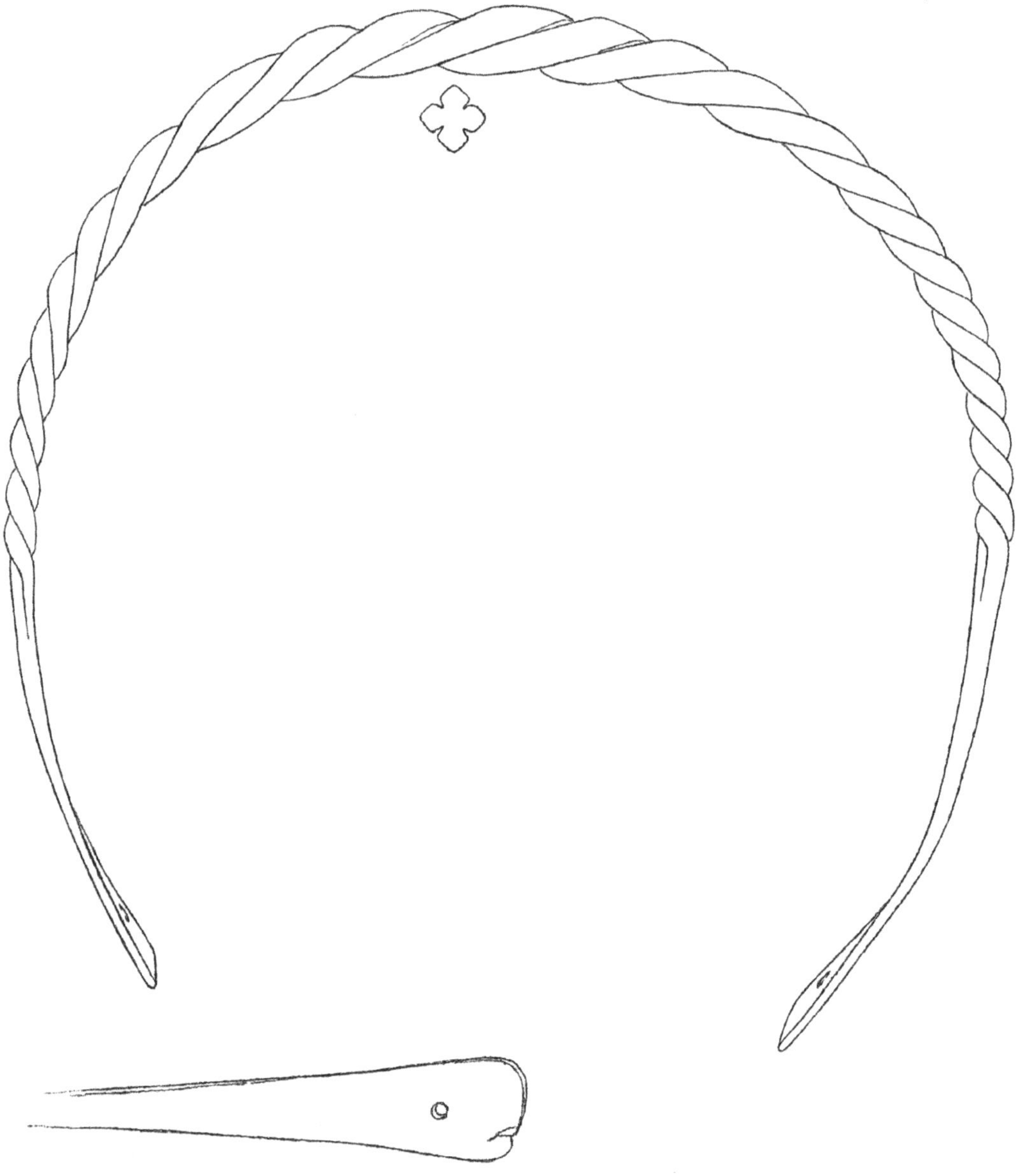

30

Remza Koščević

Plate XV

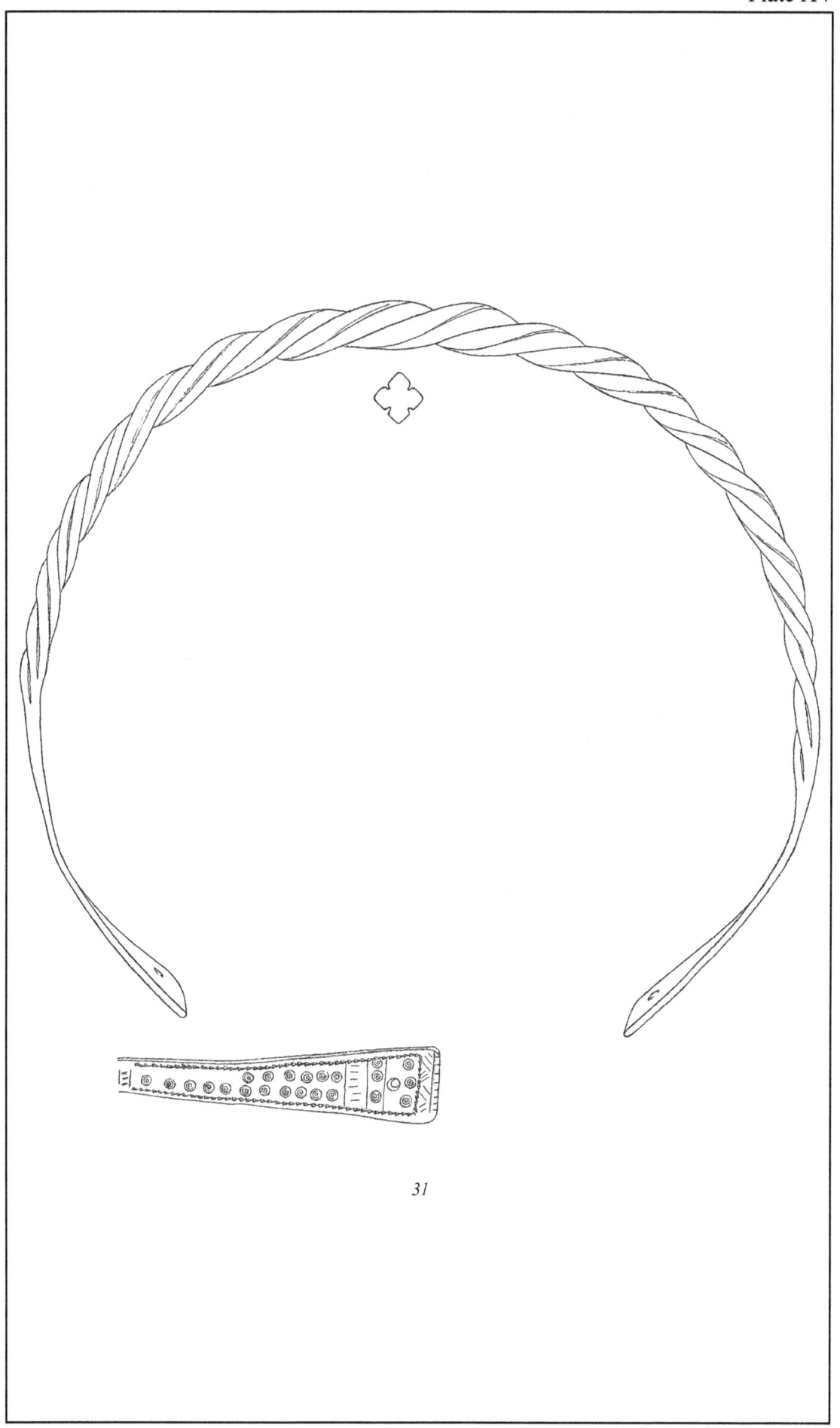

31

A Roman Hoard of Silver Jewellery

Plate XVI

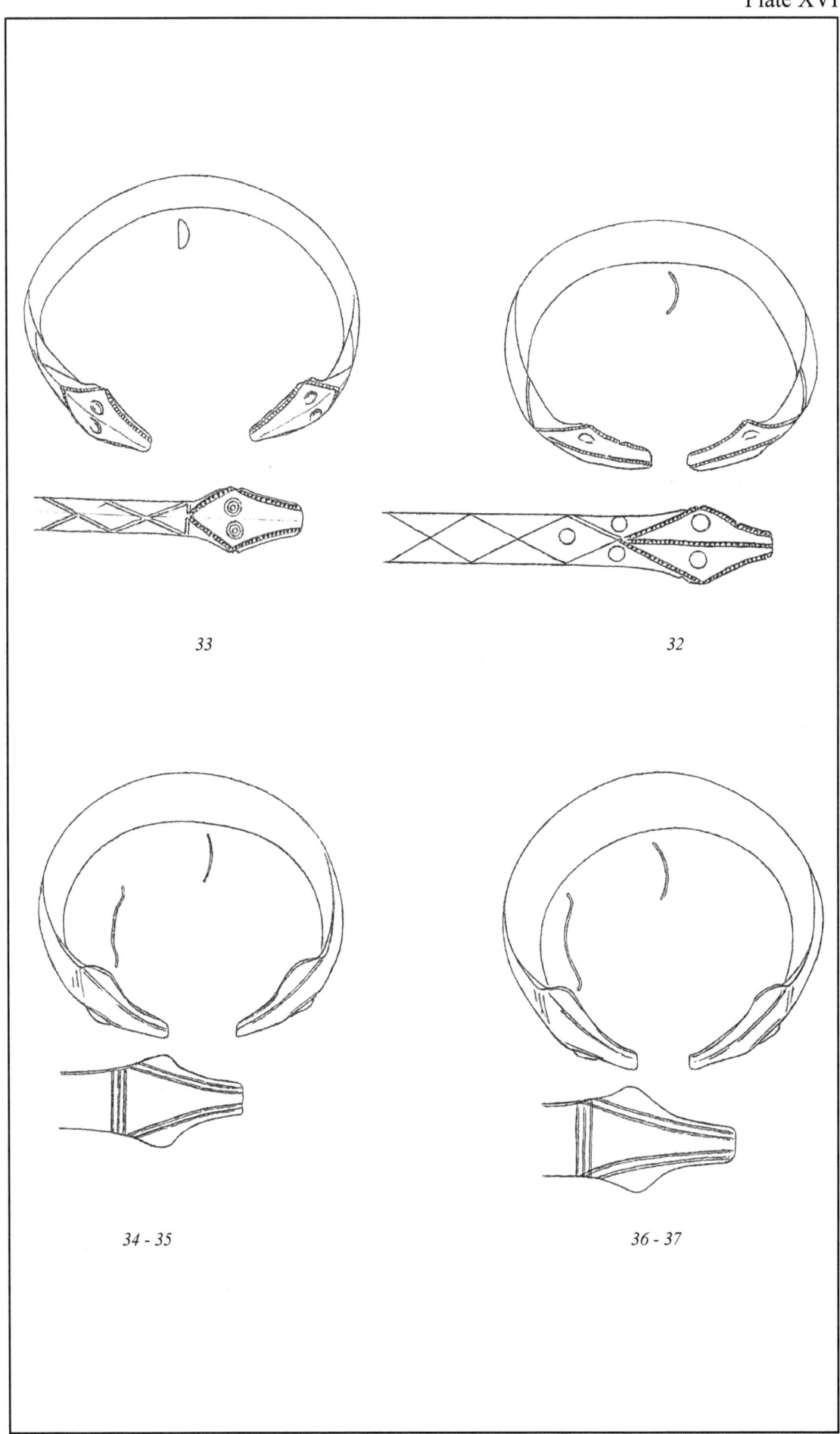

33

32

34 - 35

36 - 37

Plate XVII

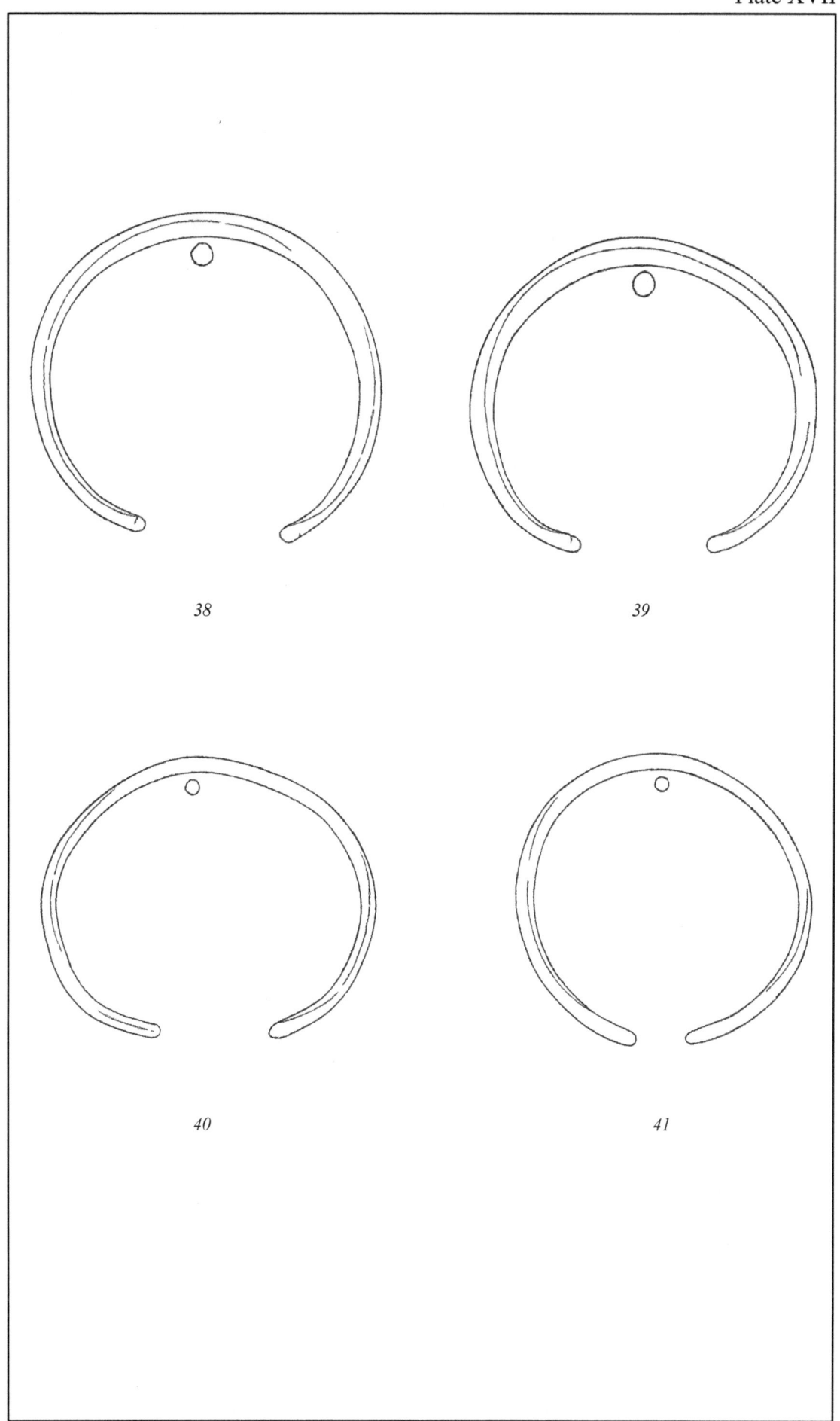

A Roman Hoard of Silver Jewellery

Plate XVIII

42

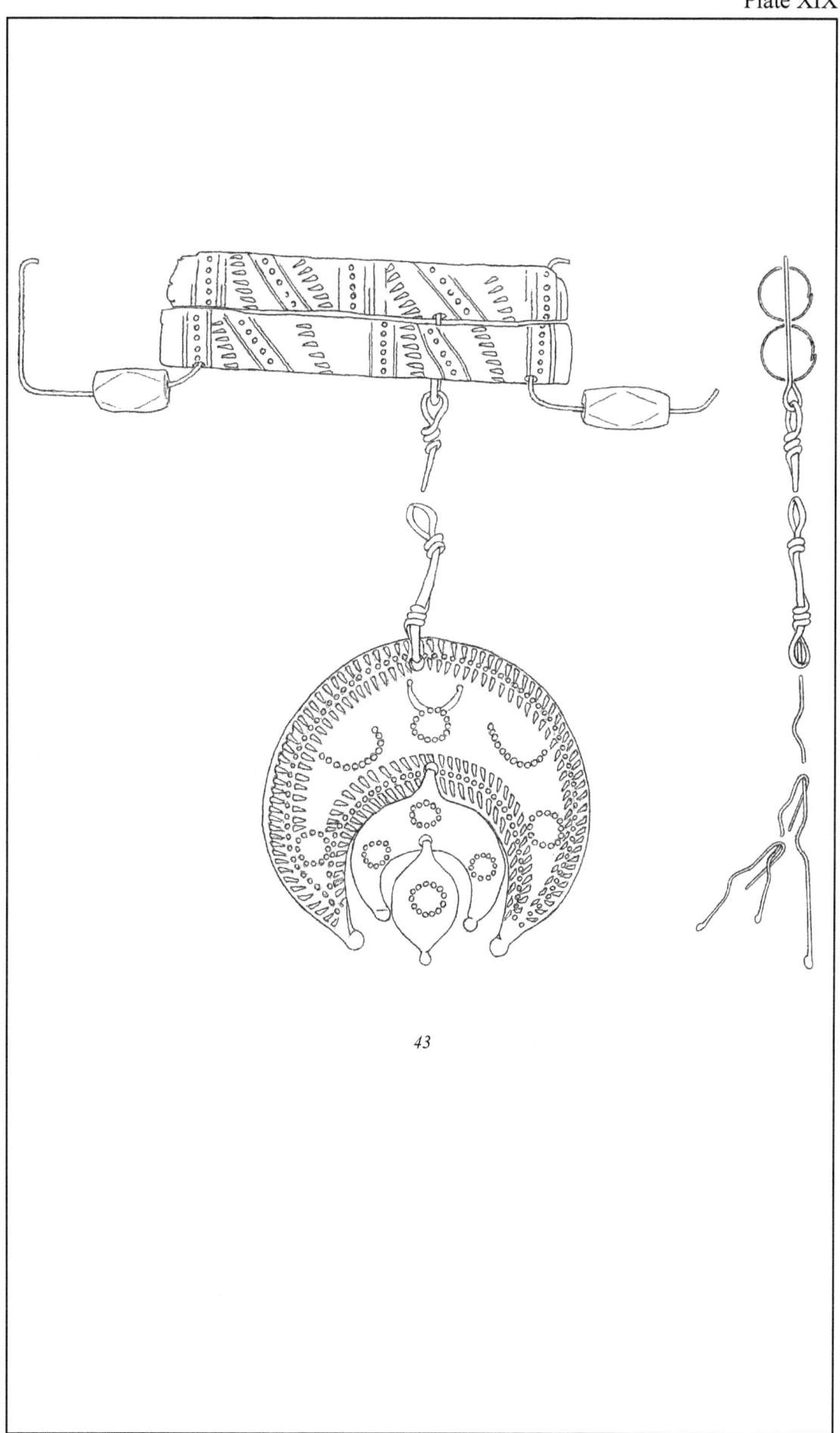

43

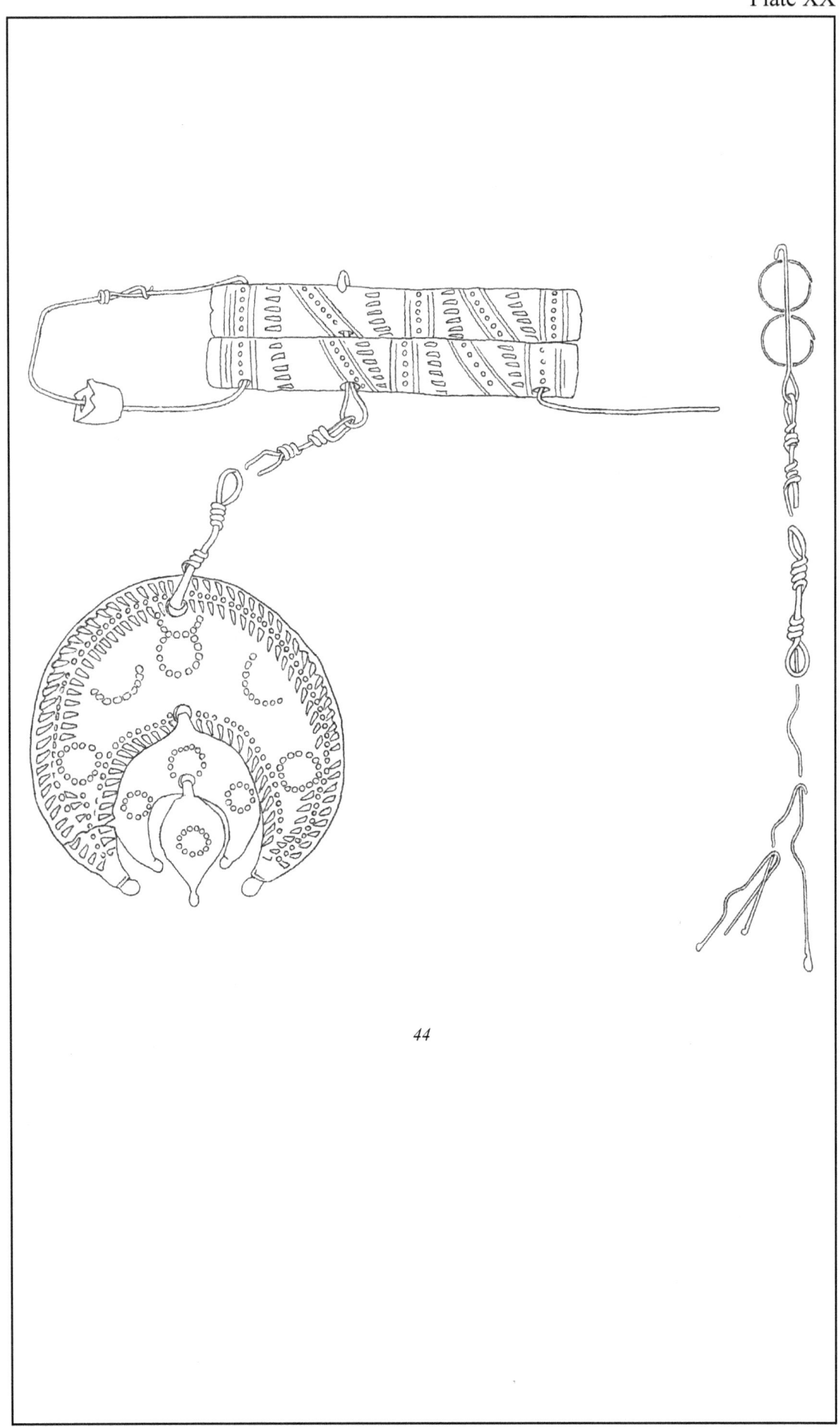

44

Remza Koščević

Plate XXI

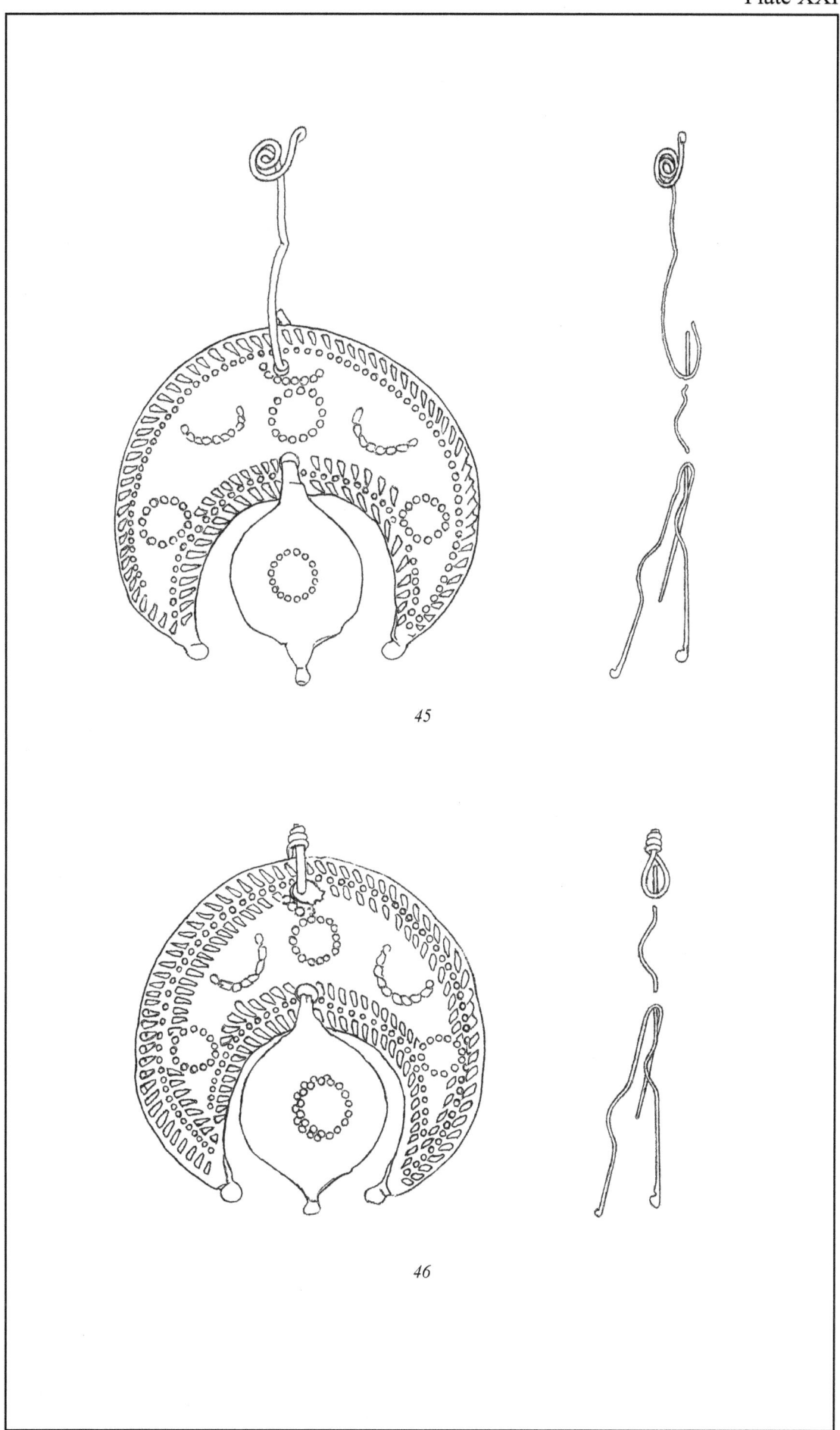

45

46

Fig. 1 a A pair of pendants (nos. 1, 2) – front

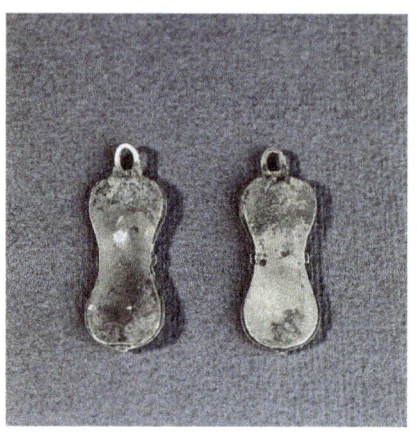

Fig. 1 b A pair of pendants (nos. 1, 2) – back

Fig. 2 a Cylindrical container (no. 3) – front

Fig. 2 b Cylindrical container (no. 4) – back

Fig. 3 a Square container (no. 5) – front

Fig. 3 b A pair of square containers (nos. 6-7) – front and side

Fig. 4 a A pair of axe-shaped pendants (nos. 8, 9) – front

Fig. 4 b A pair of axe-shaped pendants (nos. 8, 9) – back

Fig. 5 Cylindrical beads (nos. 10-18)

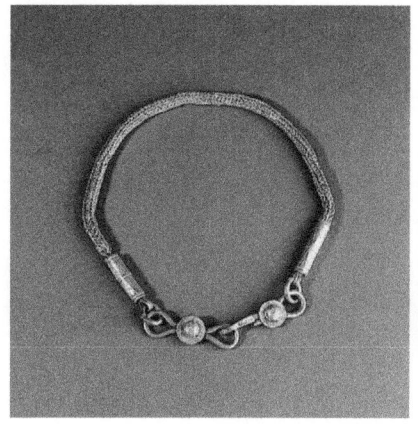

Fig. 6 a A woven chain (no. 19)

Fig. 6 b The clasps of the woven chain, no. 19

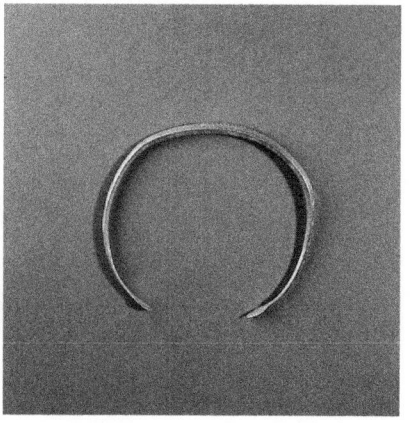

Fig. 7 a A neck ring (torc) with a smooth surface (no. 20)

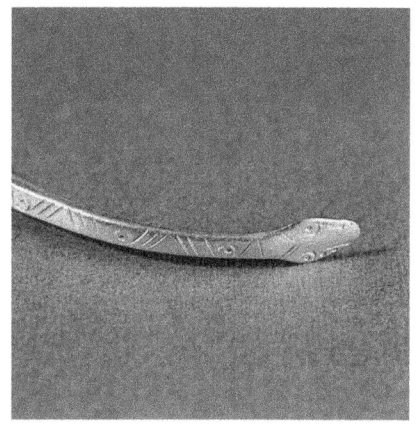

Fig. 7 b The ends of torc no. 20

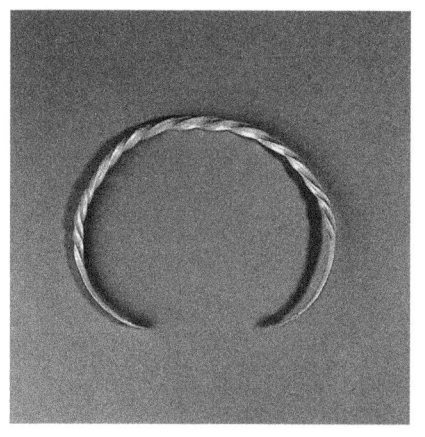

Fig. 8 a A torc with a spirally twisted surface (no. 21)

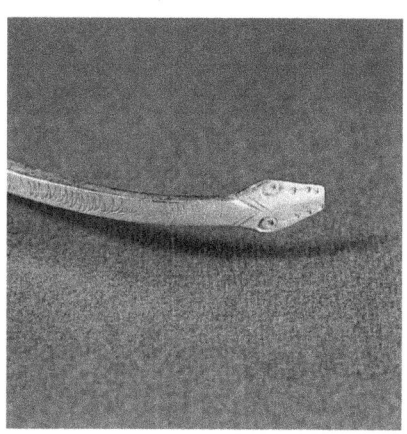

Fig. 8 b The ends of torc no. 21

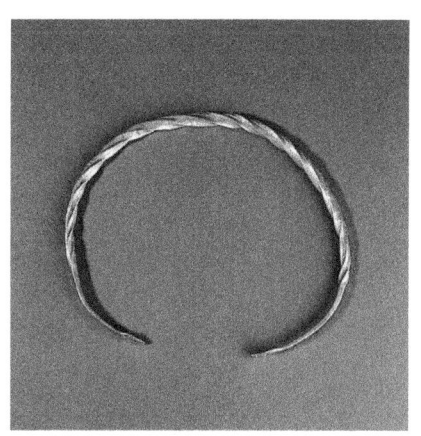

Fig. 9 a Torc (no. 22)

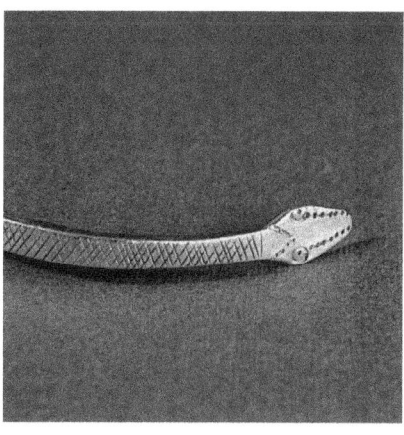

Fig. 9 b The ends of torc no. 22

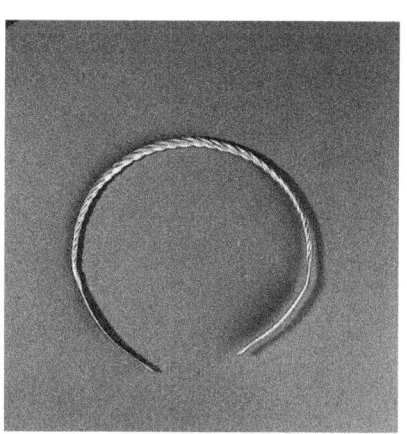

Fig. 10 a Torc (no. 23)

A Roman Hoard of Silver Jewellery

Fig. 10 b The ends of torc no. 23

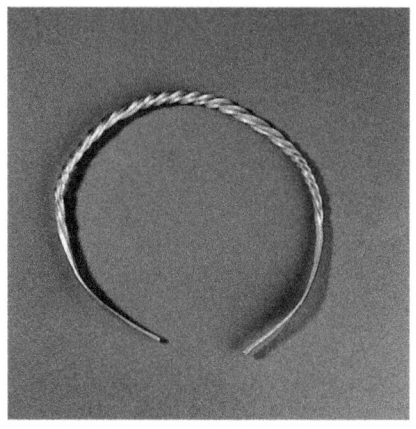

Fig. 11 a Torc (no. 24)

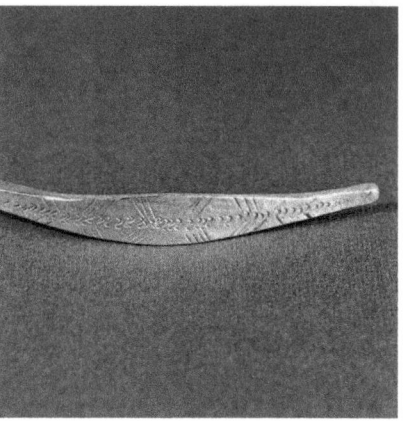

Fig. 11 b The ends of torc no. 24

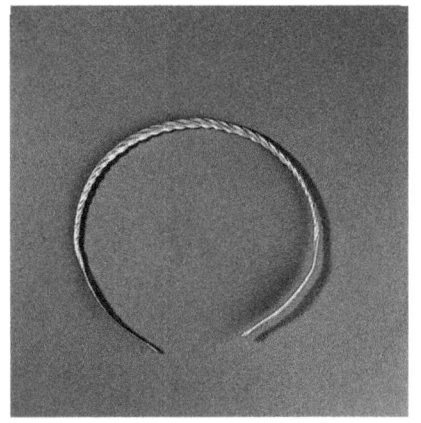

Fig. 12 a Torc (no. 25)

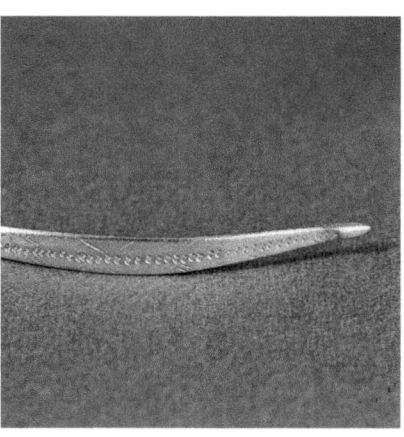

Fig. 12 b The ends of torc no. 25

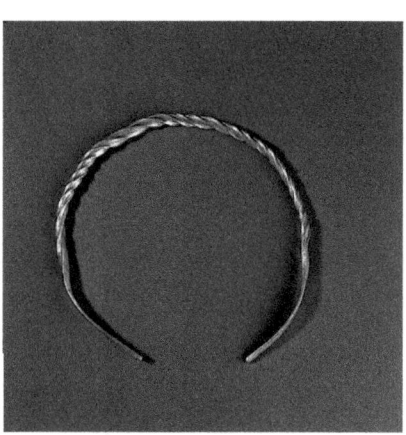

Fig. 13 a Torc (no. 26)

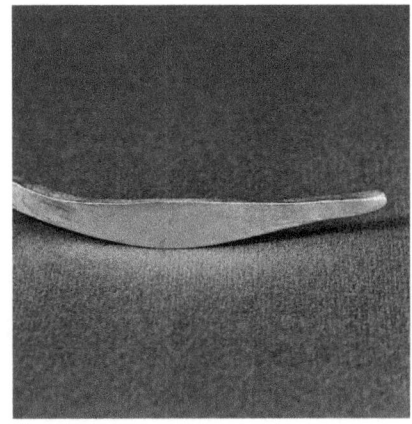

Fig. 13b The ends of torc no 26

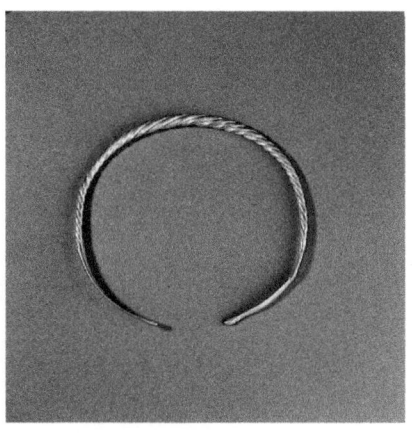

Fig. 14a Torc (no. 27)

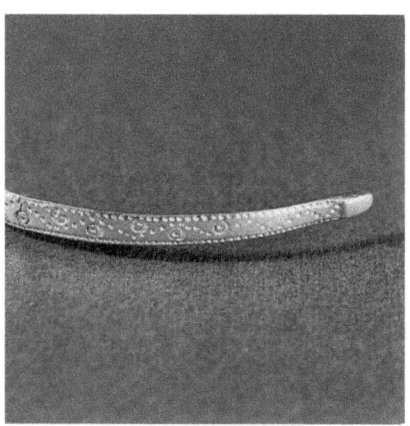

Fig. 14 b The ends of torc no. 27

Remza Koščević

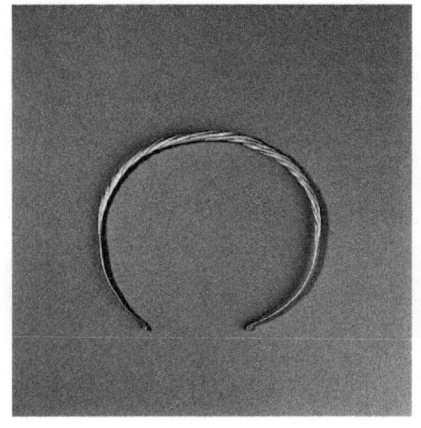

Fig. 15 a Torc (no. 28)

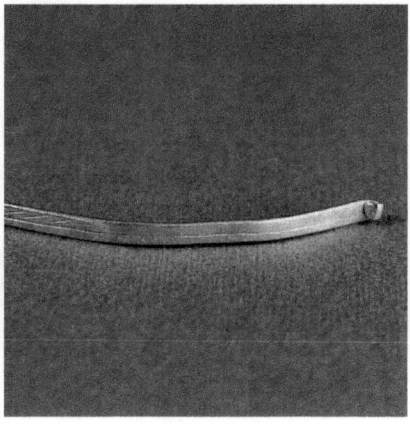

Fig. 15 b The ends of torc no. 28

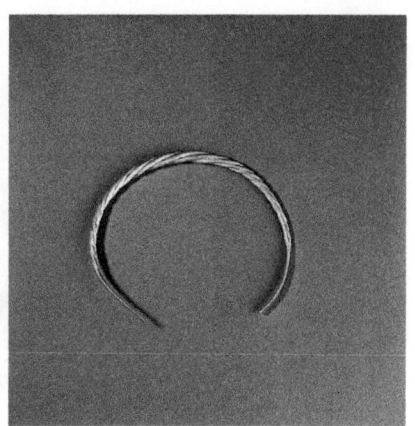

Fig. 16 a Torc (no. 29)

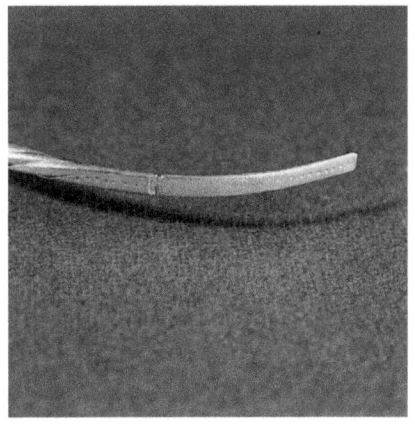

Fig. 16 b The ends of torc no. 29

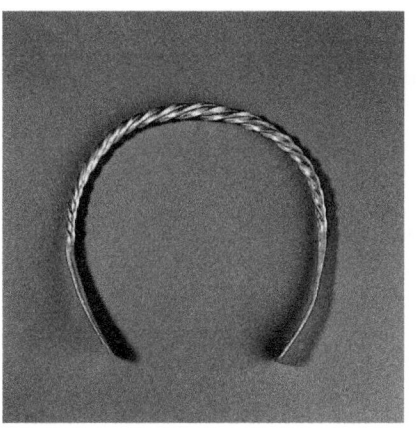

Fig. 17 a Torc (no. 30)

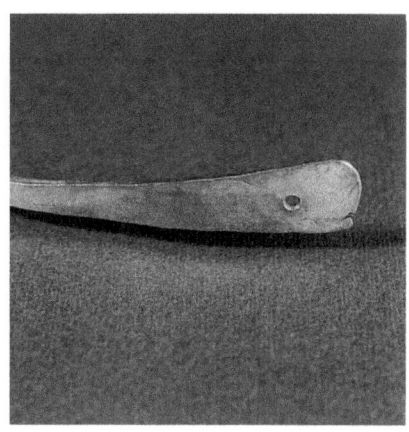

Fig. 17 b The ends of torc no. 30

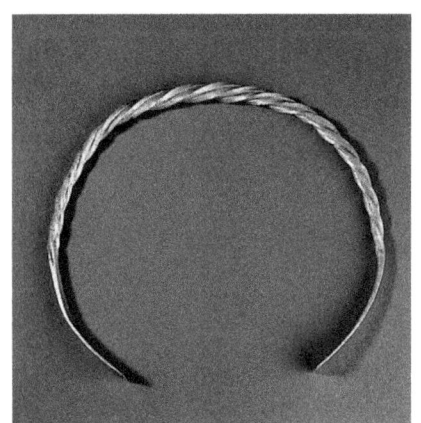

Fig. 18 a Torc (no. 31)

Fig. 18 b The ends of torc no. 31

Fig. 19 A bracelet with snake-head ends (no. 32)

Fig. 20 A bracelet with snake-head ends (no. 33)

Fig. 21 A pair of bracelets with zoomorphic ends (nos. 34, 35)

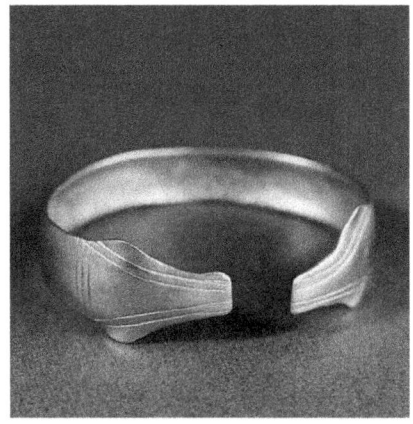

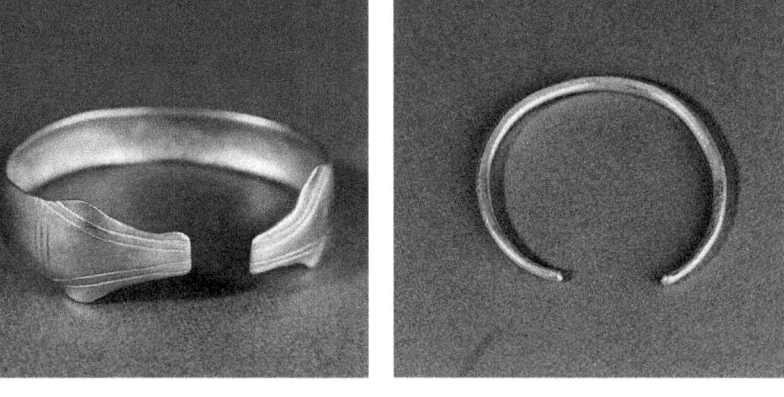

Fig. 22 A pair of bracelets with zoomorphic ends (nos. 36, 37)

Fig. 23 a Bracelet (no. 38)

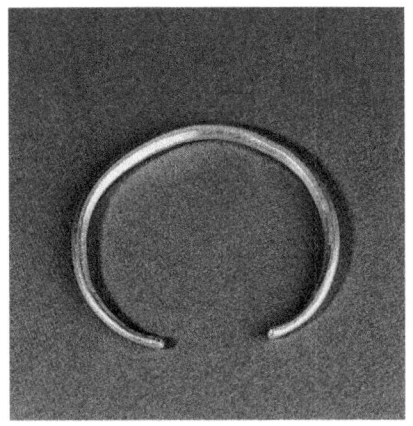

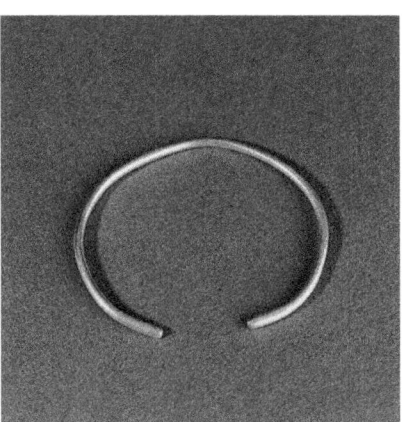

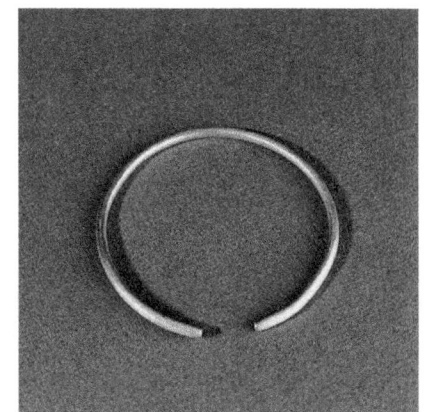

Fig. 23 b Bracelet (no. 39)

Fig. 24 A pair of bracelets (nos. 40, 41)

Fig. 25 a A tripartite crescent-shaped pendant (no. 42) – front

Fig. 25 b Pendant no. 42 – back

Fig. 26 a A tripartite crescent-shaped pendant (no. 43) – front

Fig. 26 b Pendant no. 43 – back

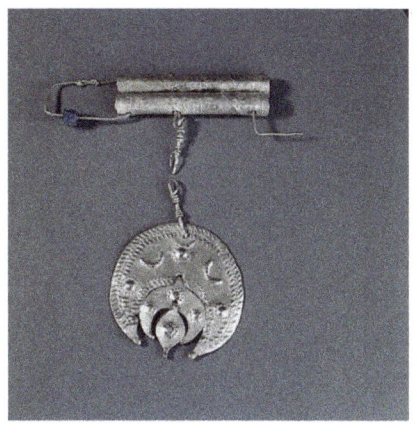

Fig. 27 A tripartite crescent-shaped pendant (no. 44)

Fig. 28 a A two-part crescent-shaped pendant (no. 45) – front

Fig. 28 b Pendant no. 45 – back

Fig. 29 A two-part crescent-shaped pendant (no. 46)

Fig. 30 The set of embossed crescent-shaped pendants (nos. 42-46)

A Roman Hoard of Silver Jewellery

 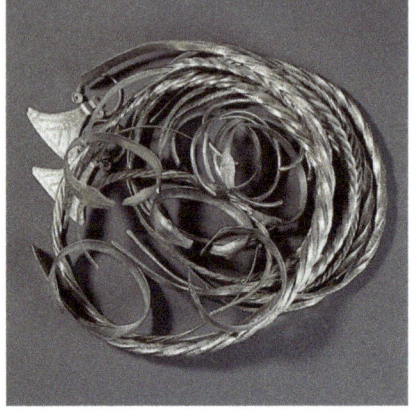 

Fig. 31 The group of a filigree/granulated items (nos. 1-7, 10-19)

Fig. 32 The group of forged items (nos. 8, 9, 20-41)

Fig. 33 The complete hoard of silver jewelery

www.ingramcontent.com/pod-product-compliance
Lightning Source LLC
Chambersburg PA
CBHW040317240426
43666CB00024B/2930